Glad Tidings

Register This New Book

Benefits of Registering*

- ✓ FREE **replacements** of lost or damaged books
- ✓ FREE **audiobook** – *Pilgrim's Progress*, audiobook edition
- ✓ FREE information about new titles and other **freebies**

www.anekopress.com/new-book-registration

*See our website for requirements and limitations.

Glad Tidings

OR, THE WAY OF LIFE

ROBERT BOYD

We enjoy hearing from our readers. Please contact us at www.anekopress.com/questions-comments with any questions, comments, or suggestions.

www.AuthorWebsite.com
Glad Tidings
© 2022 by Aneko Press
All rights reserved. First edition 1876.
Revisions copyright 2022.

Please do not reproduce, store in a retrieval system, or transmit in any form or by any means – electronic, mechanical, photocopying, recording, or otherwise, without written permission from the publisher. Please contact us via www.AnekoPress.com for reprint and translation permissions.

Scripture quotations from The Authorized (King James) Version. Rights in the Authorized Version in the United Kingdom are vested in the Crown. Reproduced by permission of the Crown's patentee, Cambridge University Press.

Cover Designer: Jonathan Lewis
Editors: Sheila Wilkinson and Ruth Clark

Aneko Press

www.anekopress.com

Aneko Press, Life Sentence Publishing, and our logos are trademarks of
Life Sentence Publishing, Inc.
203 E. Birch Street
P.O. Box 652
Abbotsford, WI 54405

RELIGION / Christian Living / Spiritual Growth

Paperback ISBN: 978-1-62245-739-7
eBook ISBN: 978-1-62245-743-4

10 9 8 7 6 5 4 3 2 1

Available where books are sold

Contents

Ch. 1: Good News 1

Ch. 2: Immanuel, God with Us 9

Ch. 3: Sinai and Calvary 17

Ch. 4: The Spirit Striving 25

Ch. 5: Saving Faith 33

Ch. 6: Obscuring Clouds 41

Ch. 7: Mighty to Save 51

Ch. 8: Peace with God 61

Ch. 9: The Thirsty Invited 69

Ch. 10: The New Creature 87

Ch. 11: Working for Jesus 97

Ch. 12: The Gospel Feast 105

Robert Boyd – A Brief Biography 129

Other Similar Titles 135

Chapter 1

Good News

There is much misunderstanding in the minds of many in regard to the word *gospel*. Some think everything they hear preached from the Bible falls under this general designation. Whether the minister is preaching on God, the immortality of the soul, or the moral duties that arise from our social relationships, it is all called preaching the gospel by such persons.

Some time ago we heard a minister preach on the subject of prayer. It was a faithful and powerful sermon. It lifted the soul up to God and made many say, "It is good to be here." At the close of the service, we heard one of the members say to another, "That was a fine gospel sermon." Now, the fact is, there was not one word of the gospel in it. A man may preach a whole year, or for a whole lifetime, and preach truth too, and yet not preach the gospel.

The celebrated Andrew Fuller (a theologian who promoted missionary work) once heard a young brother preach a sermon which might have been called eloquent and academic. When the preacher came down from the pulpit, Fuller laid his hand upon his shoulder and said, "I thank you for your sermon; it was very good, as far as it went."

"As far as it went!" said the preacher.

"Yes," said Fuller, "as far as it went, for Christ was not preached."

"But Christ was not in the text," replied the young man.

"My brother," said Fuller, "there are no side streets in this country which do not lead to the king's highway."

All the lines of truth center in Jesus, and that is a poor dry morsel of a sermon that does not contain enough of the gospel to lead an inquiring soul to pardon and peace. We greatly admire the sentiment of one of the ancient Fathers – "Were the highest heavens my pulpit, and the whole hosts of the redeemed my audience, and eternity my day, Jesus alone would be my text."

The gospel means "good news" and is a proclamation from the God of heaven to his guilty creatures on earth; for the sake of what Jesus has done, he will pardon all who trust in his faithful work and receive them as graciously as if they had never sinned at all. The good news tells of a way by which we can come to God as joyfully as Adam could before he fell. God's fatherly voice resounds to us from the heavens, saying, *This is my*

The good news tells of a way by which we can come to God as joyfully as Adam could before he fell.

beloved Son, in whom I am well pleased (Matthew 3:17). The good news is in that sentence.

Notice that the voice from heaven did not say, "*with* whom I am well pleased," though that is true. Neither does it say, "*for* whom I am well pleased," though that is also true. But it says, *in whom I am well pleased*. It is only when we see God in Christ Jesus that we can see a well-pleased God. In that one sentence, God himself preached the gospel to that awestruck multitude that stood upon the banks of the Jordan and through them to the ends of the earth.

If we approach God outside of Christ, he is a consuming fire. Let the best man that ever lived come before God with the best action he ever performed, and without Christ, God cannot be well pleased with him. His best performances are in God's pure eyes corrupted to the very core by sin. But let the vilest sinner come to God in Christ, and there is placed upon him a reconciled countenance, the smile of approval beams upon his soul with the very joy of heaven, and his eyes rise to the face of the judge as he exclaims, "Abba, Father." Indeed, a holy and a just God could bestow upon guilty man no favor, either worldly or spiritual, except through the worthiness of his Son.

A person once said, "How am I to know that Jesus died for me?"

The reply was: "Do you acknowledge that you have been a sinner all your life?"

"I do."

"And do you believe that the punishment of sin is the wrath and curse of God?"

"Yes."

"Why, then, is it that all your life you have been getting nothing from God's hand but blessings?"

This inquirer saw at once that the very sparing patience of God that had permitted him to live, and the goodness of God that covered his pathway with blessings could only come to him through the death of Jesus.

Suppose that a friend comes into your house today and says, "I have good news for you." You would understand that he had something to tell you that would make you happy. And if after he has made his statement you are not any happier than before, one of two things must be the case. Either your friend was mistaken as to the nature of the message and it was not calculated to make you happy, or else you did not believe what he said.

Now, when God sends the gospel to us, he says it is good news, that is, something intended to make us happy. If after we have heard it we are not made happy by it, either God has called something good news that wasn't, or we have not believed his Word. Yes, the only reason you are not now rejoicing in the forgiving love of God is that you have not believed his testimony concerning his Son. You can believe your fellow man when they say they have good news for you; you take up the newspaper with a face beaming with expectation when you are told there is good news for you in it. And yet, your neglected Bible lies in your houses, containing something calculated and intended to make you unspeakably happy, and you will not believe it.

It is a matter of enormous difficulty to get men to

believe that the whole work of their salvation is finished already. They will acknowledge that the favor of God is a precious thing; they will speak of making their peace with God and hope that he will be reconciled to them. But tell them of a love that has already made the peace; tell them of a grace that has already finished the salvation; tell them of a goodness so abundant and overflowing that it has absolutely left them nothing to do but to believe that all is done, and they believe you mock them. Whenever they think of becoming serious, cultivating good feelings, turning from their outward sins, and praying, they think of things that would qualify them for coming to Jesus and making God pleased with them. They forget that until they go to Jesus through faith and come to God for acceptance through the righteousness of his Son, they have not taken the very first step in true religion.

Self-righteousness, in one form or another, is a universal sin of man. Wherever man is found to exist, it reigns supreme in the unrenewed heart. The moment the sinner begins to think or speak on religion, this evil shows itself. With the light of the gospel blazing around him, and with Calvary's solemn scenes portrayed in blood before him, he still feels as if he must be accepted by God on the grounds of some good prayer, some good feelings, or some good deeds that he performs.

An imperfect obedience is just a sinful obedience.

The best obedience that man can achieve in his fallen state is imperfect. And an imperfect obedience is just a sinful obedience – a wicked obedience. Now, if God were to accept men on the grounds of such obedience, he would be virtually declaring that his law had been too strict – it had been wrong. From that moment his holy law would be impeached, it would lose its power among all intelligent beings, and its holy authority would be forever gone.

If the sinner starts for heaven on the grounds of his own imperfect righteousness, he can only get there by trampling upon the holy law of the God of heaven at every step. Allowing him at last to get there on the grounds of his own imperfect obedience, his presence would strike terror into every holy heart in heaven. The songs of that holy place would die away in groans. Its inhabitants would feel that all protection was gone, all confidence gone – if God's perfect law was gone. How, then, can the sinner hope for salvation in a way that would swallow up heaven itself in the misery of hell?

If God were to accept the sinner on the grounds of his own righteousness, he would be declaring the death of his own Son unnecessary. He would be saying that the blood of Jesus was shed in vain. He would be declaring the atonement a piece of folly – no, of absolute wickedness. The very fact that God's own Son had to die shows that nothing but a perfect righteousness would do, a righteousness so perfect that God's pure eye cannot see a single flaw in it. It shows that we needed a righteousness no less than divine, and here it is provided in Christ crucified. Abandon at once the vain attempt to make a covering for yourself by patching together the fig leaves of your own works, for in God's great name we proclaim to you the gospel's joyful sound – a righteousness unto all, and upon all, who believe.

My dear reader, if you are saved at all, you must be saved by simple faith in Christ's work. We know that the natural heart hates this doctrine and that it contradicts all of man's preconceived notions of religion. It lays pride in the dust and leaves the soul no room for boasting. Consider the holiest man now living and the vilest sinner that treads God's earth; only faith in the merits of Jesus has made the difference in them.

Suppose we had been in the city of Philippi that night when the jailer was converted (Act 16:22-34). It is the dark, midnight hour, and the city is wrapped in silence and gloom. We stand across from a gloomy-looking building, and as we gaze upon it through the darkness, it begins to heave back and forth, as if rocked in the grasp of an earthquake.

You must be saved by simple faith in Christ's work. This doctrine lays pride in the dust and leaves the soul no room for boasting.

Listen! A voice of deep human agony breaks through to our ears. It is the voice of the jailer himself, struck by the bolt of divine truth, and he says, "What shall I do to be saved?" And what are the directions which the apostles give him? Do they tell him he must pray, that he must get deeper feeling or more convictions of his sinful state, and do something to prepare himself for coming to Jesus? We find no such directions coming from the lips of these heaven-inspired men. Alas! there is no shortage in our day of professed ministers of the gospel who would give such instructions.

A minister urged an inquirer some time ago to go to the Lord's Supper. "How can I, when I have no hope in Christ?" was the reply.

"Oh, come to the Communion table, and you will feel better," said the minister.

How beautifully do the apostle's words contrast with this. *Believe on the Lord Jesus Christ, and thou shalt be saved* (Acts 16:31).

And what did the jailer do? Did he say, "That is too easy a way of being saved; it is not possible that so vile a man as I am could be saved in that way."

No, at once he believed in the Son of God as *his* Savior, and his heart was brimming over with joy. An old writer says there are but three steps to heaven:

- Out of self,
- Into Christ, and
- Into glory.

If you are not in Christ, whatever may be the outward morality of your conduct, you are condemned already, living under the curse of the law. The bolt of God's wrath may at any moment strike you. There is only one safe spot for you in the whole universe, and that is as a humble believer at the cross of Christ.

Chapter 2

Immanuel, God with Us

He that hath seen me hath seen the Father. (John 14:9)

These words came from the lips of the Lord Jesus, and there are no words like his words. They burn into the soul, for they are words of heavenly fire. Words of wisdom have been spoken by Christ's people, for the brightest intellects and the most powerful eloquence have been devoted to his service; but *never man spake like this man* (John 7:46). We can learn something of God from his works, and as we gaze upon the lofty overhanging cliff, the sky-piercing mountain, or the vast ocean, feelings of the most profound awe penetrate our being. We exclaim, "Great and infinite God!" and the cry is taken up in the heavens and re-echoed from world to world throughout infinite space.

But nature, in all her vastness, doesn't say a word

on what we, as sinners, most want to hear – pardon. Not a whisper of forgiveness comes to us from the blue heavens above us or from any of the works of God around us. The thought of the great God, girded with omnipotence, makes us afraid. We cannot comprehend the great, infinite, all-pervading Spirit. The thought of going into his presence repels rather than attracts. *I remembered God, and was troubled* (Psalm 77:3).

But when God comes near to us in human flesh, when God approaches me in the person of a man like myself, and when I hear God speaking to me through human lips, looking tenderly upon me through human eyes, shedding human tears over my wretchedness, and heaving human groans over me as he speaks of love, pardon, and adoption into his family of love, the guilty dread of God flees, and perfect love that casts out all fear takes its place. Now this is what we see in the God-man – *God was manifest in the flesh* (1 Timothy 3:16).

Suppose you entered a friend's house and saw his little children amusing themselves with that perfect enjoyment peculiar to childhood – not a frown upon their brows or a shade of sorrow on their faces. You stand and admire the lovely scene when, all at once, the father of these children is heard at the door. In a moment the whole scene changes. The children look around in terror; their faces, so recently flushed with joy, are now pale with fear, and they each hurry to hide from the father as though from an object of aversion and dread. In witnessing such a sight as this, you would know one of two things to be true: the father is either a tyrant and in the habit of abusing his children, or these children are conscious of having done wrong in his absence and, therefore, are afraid to face him.

Why does the sinner have a dread of God that makes him shun the very thought of his Creator as the essence of all that is gloomy and forbidding? Why does he dread the idea of going into God's presence and coming near the universal Father as death approaches? It cannot be because God has ever done him any wrong, for the hand that he dreads has been engaged in scattering blessings upon his pathway, and every gesture of that hand has been inviting him near. The voice he dreads to hear has been tuned to accents of love and has pleaded for him down the broad road to death – *Turn ye, turn ye . . . why will ye die?* (Ezekiel 33:11). Why, then, this despicable dread at the thought of God? Why this enmity and aversion? Ah, it is because the soul is conscious of

Man can neither love God nor enjoy happiness until this consciousness of guilt is destroyed.

guilt and of wickedly lifting the standard of rebellion against its best friend. It is because this consciousness of guilt makes him think of God as a God of wrath, the red thunderbolt whose indignation is about to leap from his right hand to destroy the sinner.

Now, man can neither love God nor enjoy happiness until this feeling is destroyed and his entire confidence in Jehovah's love is restored. We see this illustrated in our first parents. As long as they believed in God's love, they remained holy and happy. The moment they believed Satan's lie that God was selfish by keeping something from them that was good, to keep them from knowing as much as him – the very moment they believed this falsehood, they fell, and guilty dread of God took the place of confidence and love.

They had previously sent up their songs of love and joy and shared a happy harmony with the loftier songs of heaven, but are now fleeing in terror from the sound of the Lord's voice. They try to hide themselves among the trees of the garden. Why is Adam now so unhappy? As yet there is no change in his outward surroundings. The fruits are as pleasant to the taste, the flowers are as fragrant to the smell, the air as balmy, and the music of the birds as sweet as ever. His body is still in Paradise, but the very elements of hell have begun in his soul – a plain proof that no outward possessions can make man happy while his soul is estranged from the fountain of all that is good.

In *Immanuel, God with us,* we see Satan's lie fully refuted. We see the God we assumed was full of vindictive wrath coming near to us in human flesh with the tear of pity in his eye and words of inviting love upon his lips. We see that God so loved us that he stepped down from his throne at the very summit of glory and sought us on the mountains of sin. We see that we do not need to do anything to make God love us, for that love has existed all along. We do not need to do something to reconcile God to us, for whoever is in the wrong must come and be reconciled to the right; therefore, God is in Christ reconciling not himself to the world, but the world to himself.

In short, we see that as man departed from God by believing Satan's lie and disbelieving God's truth, so he must return by disbelieving Satan's lie and believing God's truth. And as he lost his happiness when he lost his confidence in God's seeming disinterested love, so he can never regain his happiness until he believes in that love as displayed in Christ Jesus. Thus it is written, *Acquaint now thyself with him and be at peace* (Job 22:21). And again, *They that know thy name will put their trust in thee* (Psalm 9:10). That is, the moment they really *know God,* as he is revealed in the gospel, that moment they are at peace with him. But a man may know about God and yet not know God. He may be a profound theologian and be able to speak eloquently about the attributes of God, and yet know no more of him in the true spiritual sense than a Hottentot, an indigenous nomadic herdsman of South Africa. To know God is to know him as the forgiving Father, and this he can only know through Jesus Christ his Son.

In light of this, how important the doctrine of Christ's divinity appears! Take that truth out of the Bible, and you shatter humanity's lifeboat to pieces and leave man a miserable wreck upon the shores of eternity. This is the foundation of the bridge that crosses the gulf of human despair. If it is taken away, the whole structure falls to pieces. Rejecting the divinity of Christ is the most dangerous error that has ever cursed our world, for it strikes at the root of the atonement, the only hope for man. Therefore, when unbelievers attempt to destroy Christianity under the most plausible arguments, they begin by denying the divinity of Christ.

If someone with great power desired to destroy our solar system, it would not be necessary to go from orb to orb, destroying one after another. It would only be necessary to dash out the sun, and our whole solar system would rush wildly into one mass of ruin. Some men who call themselves Christians have taken away our Lord's divinity and thus removed the life and power of the whole Christian system. But they cannot impose the dead body for the living form on the devout soul. When they talk of Christ, it is not the Christ of the Bible they speak of, but a Christ formed in their own vain imaginations. However much they may extol him as a good and virtuous man, the believer says, "You have taken away my Lord, and I know not where you have laid him."

The tears of Jesus over your perishing state show how fearful your peril is.

Sinner! In the tears and sufferings of the God-man, see how great your danger is. The tears of Jesus over your perishing state, and the deep anxieties of his soul for your salvation show how fearful your peril is. You are out in a steamboat on the lake, enjoying a pleasure excursion on a lovely summer day. There is not a cloud in the sky nor a ripple upon the waters. The calmness of the lake reflects all that is bright and beautiful in the firmament above. The thought of danger never crosses your mind, and you are sinking into sweet enjoyment of the whole scene, when suddenly you see the excited captain rush across the deck with tears rolling down his cheeks. You also see the crew deeply affected, and you at once begin to think there must be danger near, though you cannot see it.

Now, when we see God in human form weeping and

bleeding for sinners, there must be some fearful peril – there must be some deep damnation on the brink of toppling your soul! Oh, go at once to the Captain of our salvation and cry, "Lord save me, or I perish!" – and the hand that bears the print of the nail while guiding the stars in their courses will pluck you from destruction and give you a place among his loved ones on earth and among his redeemed in heaven in the end. But remember that the same hand that is strong to save is also strong to strike. The feet of those who have carried others to their burial may be at the door to entomb you. The shuttle may have passed the loom and woven the last garment in which your cold corpse is to be enshrouded, and this night your soul may stand before God. Dear reader, would you dare to stand there in a Christless state? That holy presence would be as a consuming fire to your guilty soul.

Chapter 3

Sinai and Calvary

He that believeth not is condemned already. (John 3:18)

It is not necessary for the man without Christ to wait until his death or the day of judgment to be condemned, for he is under the curse of the law now, and the curse of the law is the curse of God. Go where he will, do what he may, that curse is upon him. He may banish the remembrance of it from his thoughts; he may plunge into scenes of festive and fashionable recreation; he may immerse his mind in the cares and perplexities of business. He may roam through the fields of literature and art and expand his intellect in the wonderful revelations of science. But, engage himself as he may, the sentence of death has gone forth against him, and the execution of that sentence is only delayed to afford him an opportunity of going to Christ for pardon and eternal life.

When he lies upon his bed at night, that curse surrounds him like a curtain; when he walks far and near, it is his attendant; and when he laughs in the theater, in the barroom, or at a festive occasion, that tremendous curse frowns in wrath over his head. The law says, *Cursed is every one that continueth not in all things which are written in the book of the law to do them* (Galatians 3:10). Now, dear reader, if you can show that since the moment that you became a responsible being to the present time you have never sinned in thought, word, or deed, or that you have loved God with all your heart and your neighbor as yourself during your whole life, then you are not under the curse. You can claim eternal life as a right, according to the terms of the law: "Do and live."

Your conscience testifies, however, that you have not lived a perfectly holy life, and the need for this perfect holiness brings this curse upon you. No man will ever go to Christ for a blessing until he feels himself burdened with this curse. The hoarse, stern voice of justice must be heard from Sinai, pronouncing our condemnation, before we will listen to the *still small voice* of love from Calvary, declaring our justification. It is in vain that you push food upon a man who is not hungry, or offer charity to one who thinks he is rich and increasing in possessions. Until the soul feels its lost and hopeless condition, there will be no music in the name Jesus and no attraction in Calvary. The sinner must understand that God cannot permit his law to be trampled upon with immunity from punishment, and that sin is the most fearful thing in the whole universe. If it is pardoned, it can only be blotted out through the untold sufferings of God's own Son, but if unpardoned, it must be followed by an eternity of anguish.

Upon visiting France, a German prince went to see the place where many convicts were confined. In tribute to his rank, he was permitted to recognize his visit by giving one of the convicts their liberty. He spoke to one man, whose intelligent look attracted him, and asked him for what crime he was imprisoned. In reply the convict told him the most unlikely story of his innocence and of how false witnesses had sworn against him.

God cannot permit his law to be trampled upon with immunity from punishment.

The prince left him and put the same question to another, who also denied his guilt and declared that he had been mistaken for another man. The same question was put to several others with the same result until at last the prince came to a man whose solemn and gloomy countenance attracted his attention. The man's reply was: "I have been a vile wretch and have deserved far more than my present punishment. I have openly defied the laws of both God and men and am not fit to look upon God's blue heavens or the green earth."

The prince, turning to his attendants, said, "Set this man free; he is in a fit state of mind to make a proper use of his liberty."

Likewise the Prince of Peace receives and pardons the sinner when he is in a state of mind that justifies

God and condemns himself. When the pride of the soul is broken, the sinner ceases to look at himself in the mirror of the world's notions and standards, which make the most deformed person look attractive in their own eyes. But he now looks at himself in the mirror of God's law, and the result is that he sees himself more like God sees him, and abhors himself, and repents in dust and ashes (Job 42:6).

We have an illustration of the truth of these remarks in the religious history of the apostle Paul. He says, *I was alive without the law once: but when the commandment came, sin revived, and I died* (Romans 7:9). He stood high in his own estimation. He thought he was in high favor with God – as good as any of his acquaintances and better than most. He tells us that the reason for this good opinion of himself was that he was *without the law*. This does not mean that he was without the knowledge of the law, for, doubtless, from the time he was a child he could repeat the law of God correctly.

But it means that he was ignorant of the far-reaching spirituality of God's law, extending as it does to the thoughts and feelings of the heart. He could point to one commandment after another and proudly say, "I have never broken any of them." And so far as the outward act is concerned, this was probably true, but he forgot that the revengeful thought is murder, the covetous thought is theft, and the impure thought is adultery. He forgot that it is futile to go through a heartless round of religious ceremonies if love for God is not the grand motivating power that governs our lives. Hence, when the spirituality of the law flashed upon his mind, in the light of a new conviction, his own words were: *the commandment came, sin revived, and I died.* Then the sins of his whole life appeared before him, unpardoned, black in their intensification, and loudly calling for God's wrath upon his head. His hope perished; his delusion was torn away; the foundation that he had built upon the sand lay around him, a pile of ruins. Sin seemed *exceeding sinful* (Romans 7:13).

Like a self-satisfied man who considered himself rich with accumulated possessions, when he put his hand into his pocket to pull out his stuffed purse, his fingers touched the slimy folds of a loathsome serpent instead. With loathing and disappointment, he would draw back his hand. Like a man who supposes himself well dressed and is on the way to attend a festive and fashionable party, when he enters the well-lit room and the scrutiny of a hundred eyes is on him, he looks at himself and finds that he is covered with *filthy rags.* With shame and confusion, he'd shrink away.

So it was with Paul when he saw the purity of God's law and felt himself the object of its terrible curse. When he was thus emptied of self, he was in a state to be filled with Christ; and when his false hope went out in darkness, the hope in Jesus that *maketh not ashamed* arose in imperishable splendor within his soul (Romans 5:5). In his own words, the law was a *schoolmaster* to bring him to Christ.

We see, then, that the reason many are boasting of their morality and wrapping themselves up in a self-righteous security is that they measure themselves by a false standard of their own making. And until they can be induced to abandon that false measure and measure themselves by the perfect purity of God's law, the cross of Christ will appear as foolishness to them, and those truths that fill all heaven with rapture will fall upon their ears as the whistling of the empty wind.

For example, a man might think that all God requires of him is to live a strictly moral life. To be honest in his dealings with his fellow man, to be kind and compassionate to the suffering and the destitute, to be a good citizen and faithfully fulfill the relative duties of life – this is his standard of duty, and he at least on some level achieves it. He is a fairly honest man. He is a generally kind neighbor, a reasonably good husband, a mostly affectionate father. He has respect for religion and for its ministers. He goes to the house of God regularly and contributes to the support of the gospel. In short, he lives up to his own standard of what a Christian should be in every respect, and the result is that he feels at peace. No disturbing doubt alarms him. He is *alive without the law* (Romans 7:9).

Men like to hear God's warnings spoken in a way that never touches their consciences.

Such a man can never be converted or repent and believe in Christ until he measures himself by a different standard. Such a man may like to hear the most faithful preaching because he is persuaded that it does not refer to him. And men like to hear the condemnation of things that they never will identify with themselves. They like to hear God's warnings spoken in a way that never touches their consciences. They like practical preaching that does not rebuke them.

Some years ago I met a man who may illustrate the above remarks. In the course of a conversation on religious subjects, I asked him if he was a Christian. He seemed astonished at the question, but promptly replied that he was. I then asked him how long it was since the great change had taken place. He replied that his parents had been good Christian people; that in his infancy he had been baptized into the true church; that he regularly received communion from the hands of the minister; and that he did not know what I meant by *the great change.*

I told him that, though it was a privilege to be born of devout parents, the religion of heaven was not hereditary – not a thing that ran in the blood. I explained that his belonging to the true church could not save him, for Judas outwardly belonged to the true church and yet went to hell. I further pointed out that his baptism could not save him, for Simon was baptized by the hands of an inspired apostle and yet had *neither part nor lot in this matter* (Acts 8:21). I read the conversation of our Lord with Nicodemus to him and urged him to have a change of heart.

He became very solemn and said he knew that he had not paid attention to these things as he ought, but of late he had become a changed character. He told me that for the last few weeks he had read three chapters out of the Bible and prayed three times every day; and, if that was not religion, he did not know what it was. I tried to show him the purity and far-reaching nature of God's law – that as a sinner the curse of the law was upon him. I explained that, though he could begin from that moment and live a perfectly holy life until the moment of his death, even then he could not be saved, for his past sins, in all their condemning power, would still convict him. I tried to lead him to Calvary for salvation, pointing him to a finished work that his own good works, prayers, and tears could add nothing to. I told him at that moment there was nothing between him and forgiveness but his own unbelief. I urged him to believe that Jesus died for him as if he had been the only sinner in the world. He received the testimony of God and was soon able to say with Paul, *[He] loved me, and gave himself for me* (Galatians 2:20).

Chapter 4

The Spirit Striving

A thoughtless sinner – it is hard to conceive of a more somber sight. He faces the certainty of soon standing in the presence of a holy God with innumerable sins staining his soul, not one of which he can wash away. His soul is more valuable than he can imagine, and there will be suffering or rejoicing when suns and systems have gone to the general pile of ruin. He stands with responsibilities under which an angel might tremble – utterly careless.

The great God has taken such a deep interest in his welfare that for a time he emptied heaven of the loveliest object in it and sent his Son on a mission of love to the perishing millions of our race. The Son so loved him that he endured the agonies of the cross and refused to come down until he had finished the work of human redemption. The Holy Spirit has such an interest in this man that, though he hates his sins with a perfect hatred, he still follows him with appeals of love. The holy angels take such an interest in him that they watch for his repentance, and yet, there he is, careless about himself!

But when the sinner begins to think, to look eternity and all its awful realities in the face, his case is truly hopeful. When a young man is taken out of a river, supposedly drowned, the physician uses every means to restore his life. The mother of that youth hangs over him in an agony of suspense. When at last they see the first signs of returning life, the fluttering of the heart, the quivering of the eyelids, and the heaving of the deep groan, that mother clasps her hands, and turning her tearful eyes to heaven, she cries, "Thank God, he lives."

The Bible describes us as *dead in trespasses and sins* (Ephesians 2:1). This is true not only of the most depraved sinners but also of the most amiable and moral sinner. Death appears in different forms – sometimes horrid and revolting and sometimes lovely and attractive. If you look over the battlefield when the conflict is over, you will see death in some of its most revolting forms. However, if you gaze upon a mother who holds a lifeless baby, its peaceful appearance is seen as a most attractive quality. But the man slain in battle and the babe are both equally dead.

Only the Holy Spirit can speak life into the dead soul.

Only the Holy Spirit can speak life into the dead soul. All the faithful ministers of the gospel and all the praying people who hold up their arms in emotional appeals might gather around one sinner and try to save that soul. They might continue their efforts for years, but they cannot produce one good thought or one saving response without the influence of the Holy Spirit.

Dear reader, if this divine Agent has touched your soul to produce some signs of spiritual life, you are in a very solemn and critical time. You cannot remain in this state for long, for you will allow the Spirit to lead you to the Lord Jesus for pardon and peace, or you will resist him and slip back into a state of a more hardened heart. This crisis – a turning point of your soul – serves to encourage you to become a Christian more than ever before or, perhaps, more than ever again.

The Spirit has startled your soul from its long and deathlike apathy. The people of God pray for you and try to point you to the Lamb of God. The Word preached from the pulpit now sounds as it never did before – pointed, personal, and solemn – but as the blast of the last trumpet, it reaches your trembling heart with an awakening *Thou art the man* (2 Samuel 12:7). You remember the pages of your past life – the sins you have committed, the prayers and counsels of a devoted mother that you have despised, and the Sabbaths you have squandered. These all speak to you in words of rebuke that you hear through every chamber of your soul. Now is the most opportune time you will ever have to accept the offers of the gospel!

But if you resist the Spirit, your mind will be darkened to the things of God; the things relating to your personal salvation will be regarded with a sullen indifference. God will say, "He is attached to his idols; let him alone." Of all the calamities that can happen to the soul on this side of judgement, to be left alone is the most terrible.

When the benevolent monks who reside in the Alps go out in the snowstorm to search for travelers who, overcome by fatigue and cold, have sunk down to perish, they always know when they come to a person whose case is hopeless. He is very hard to wake, and when they do partially rouse him, he is very disturbed and insists on being allowed to remain where he is. So it is with those gospel-hardened sinners who have long resisted the Spirit and whose souls are bound up in the chains of a mighty lethargy. When a revival sweeps through a whole community and enters the very house where such a man lives, he slumbers on in indifference or becomes a deadly adversary. He even glories in his shame and boasts of how calm he can be in the general excitement.

But the calm he boasts of is like that fearful calm we sometimes see in nature, when a storm is brewing in the heavens, about to break forth in destructive power. This calm is what the sick man feels when the inflammation that tortures his body has turned into degeneration. He thinks he is better, and his friends congratulate him on his improvement; but the physician looks gloomy, for he knows that soon his heart will be struggling wildly under the attack of death. So the sinner has resisted the Spirit, until his convictions have all left him, and he cries, "Peace and safety," when destruction is thundering at his door.

The great sin that the Spirit comes to convince us of is the sin of unbelief. The Lord's own words are: *When he is come, he will reprove the world of sin, . . . of sin, because they believe not on me* (John 16:8-9). It was not enough that Jesus died for the guilty and made salvation as free as the air we breathe or as the mountain torrent, leaping from rock to rock. Such is the deep depravity of the human heart that not one of the whole race would have believed in this boundless love if the Holy Spirit had not come to convince them of unbelief. I know of nothing that shows more clearly the extent of our hopeless, lost state than this – that it needed not only God in our nature to die for us, but it also needs God the Spirit to convince us that we need such a Savior at all.

> *Our hopeless, lost state needed not only God to die for us, but it also needs God to convince us that we need a Savior at all.*

The proper definition of *unbelief* as given by the Bible is truly fearful. It is described as making God a liar. Suppose your truthfulness was doubted by all those around you day after day, and your family, your neighbors, and the persons with whom you do business every day were to turn away from your words as not worth believing. How bitter you would feel! What indignation would fill your heart! Then, how must the great God feel when the very creatures for whom he has done so much – for whom he has made infinite sacrifices – refuse to believe his words and cast them back in his face with contempt! Is it any wonder that the unalterable decree has gone forth from the eternal throne – *He that believeth not shall be damned* (Mark 16:16)?

But it is not often that spoken unbelief will contradict God. Occasionally some bold blasphemer may dare to do this, but generally the unbelief of the heart will assume a more hypocritical and, therefore, a more dangerous form. As Satan transforms himself into an angel of light, so the sin of unbelief will often come disguised with the most profound humility. It will say, "I am too great a sinner for Christ to pardon me." This is a sham humility and has its origin in an *evil heart of unbelief, in departing from the living God* (Hebrews 3:12).

Suppose the mayor of this city were to issue a proclamation, calling upon all the destitute poor to come to his office to receive free bread, *without money and without price* (Isaiah 55:1). But, suppose in passing along the street that day I see a man weeping bitterly, who informs me he is starving. I show him the proclamation and point him to the office where he can get immediate relief. But he says, "I am too hungry to get anything; the proclamation cannot mean those who are as hungry as I am!" Why, we would think the man was mad if we heard him speak in this way. We would tell him that his hunger and destitution formed his only qualification for coming.

And this is what the Spirit seeks to impress upon the mind of the awakened sinner. He tells him that his sins, which he uses as a reason for staying away from Christ, are his only qualifications for coming to him. An awakened sinner was once lamenting his sins in the presence of Lady Huntington, and in the bitterness of his soul, he cried out, "I am lost."

"I am glad to hear it," said the pious lady.

"What," said he, "glad to hear that I am lost?"

"Yes," was the reply, "*for the Son of man came to seek and to save that which was lost*" (Luke 19:10). The Holy Spirit took that word and applied it to his heart; he saw that the cause of his despondency was unbelief, and he immediately received Christ by faith, *and he went on his way rejoicing* (Acts 8:39).

Another reason the Spirit seeks to convince us of unbelief is that this is the damning sin and the cause of every other sin. Why is a man a swearer, a drunkard, a Sabbath-breaker, or an open transgressor of the law of God? It is because he has not believed with the heart on the Son of God. The moment the soul believes, faith works by love and purifies the heart. The Spirit of God does not seek to induce the sinner to cut off this outward sin and another outward sin, leaving the great root of all sin in the heart untouched.

> *The moment the soul believes, faith works by love and purifies the heart.*

This would be like a man who wanted to cut down a tree and began with his knife at the top branches; he worked his way down, instead of laying the axe at the root of the tree at once. The Spirit lays the axe of Christ's truth at the root of the tree of unbelief, and immediately the man becomes *a new creature* in Christ Jesus (2 Corinthians 5:17). The principle of love for him who died for him becomes the controlling and impelling motive. He works, not *for* life, but because he *has* life. Heaven is not merely *before* him, it is also *within* him.

Remember, then, that whatever may be your

convictions and your terrors, whatever may be the number of your prayers, tears, and good resolutions, until you come to Jesus and cast yourself wholly on him, you are resisting the Spirit. You are in a state of unbelief and in danger of being called into the presence of God, who has pronounced a fearful sentence against this sin.

> Dwell, therefore, in our hearts;
>   Our minds from bondage free;
> Then shall we know, and praise; and love
>   The Father, Son, and Thee.[1]

---

[1] Joseph Hart, "Come, Holy Spirit, Come," 1759.

Chapter 5

Saving Faith

Faith in Jesus is essential to eternal life. A man can be saved without knowing many of the important truths in the Bible. He may get to heaven without being a Presbyterian, a Methodist, or a Baptist, but heaven's gates will be forever barred against him if he dies without faith in Jesus. This is not *a* way of being saved; it is *the* way. All that makes heaven happy, all that makes hell miserable, depends on our reception or rejection of this truth.

A man may say he will have nothing to do with this truth, but it will have something to do with him. He may assume the position of proud neutrality, but Jesus declares such neutrality impossible. *He that is not with me is against me* (Matthew 12:30). The death of Jesus throws the soul of man into a new dispensation. It is his only hope, his only way of escape from the ruin in which he is involved. The gospel meets him as he lands upon the shores of time, and it will prove to be the savior of life or of death. It will leave him in the undefiled brightness of heaven or in the hopeless misery of the lost.

In the Bible, truths are made plain in proportion to their vital importance. Deep mysterious truths that are hard to understand can be found in that Holy Book, but the plan of salvation is not hard to understand. Indeed, it is so simple and plain that thousands are stumbling into hell over its very simplicity. Instead of believing in the death of the Son of God for justification and eternal life, they are looking for some mysterious influence to come down from heaven, charge them like an electrical shock, and fill them with unspeakable delight. They are waiting for some wonderful light to break into their dark minds, and some mysterious voice to tell them that they are forgiven. Now faith in Jesus is not merely to believe that he is the Son of God who died to save sinners – that he has made a perfect atonement for the guilty. It is more than knowing that he is able and willing to save all who come unto him and that his blood is sufficient to cleanse us from all sin. A man may believe all this, just as the devil believes it but remains unsaved, for his may only be the assent of the intellect to perceived truth. The mind may be convinced of the truthfulness of God's testimony, but that testimony exerts no saving influence on the heart.

But when a man really comes to Jesus, he recognizes himself as a poor, lost, undone sinner – conscious that

> *The mind may be convinced of the truthfulness of God's testimony, but that testimony exerts no saving influence.*

he can do nothing to save himself or improve his condition, trusting wholly in the work on the cross for his acceptance with the Father. True faith makes a close, personal matter of the death of Jesus. It says, "He died not only for sinners but also for me, the chief of sinners." It says, "In myself I am nothing, but Jesus died for my sins, and through his righteousness I know I am accepted."

True faith takes God at his word. It sets before its eyes the awful scene on Calvary, the sinking head, the gushing blood, the open wounds, the dying words of the Son of God. It remembers that the Father is well pleased with the Son and his work, and through his finished work, he can be just and the justifier of the ungodly.

The man who thus believes in Jesus knows he is forgiven, not because he has been told in a dream or had it whispered to his soul by some mysterious voice, or flashed upon his mind by some sudden impression, but simply because God says it. To trust in my own impressions, feelings, and emotions is sheer fanaticism, but to trust in the testimony of God concerning his Son is highly rational. It is to be able to give a reason for the hope that is in us. Surely there can be no firmer foundation upon which an immortal soul can rest its hopes than the word of that God who cannot lie.

Suppose you had offended a dear friend by your bad conduct, and knowledge of that friend's displeasure had become very grievous to you – a burden you could no longer bear. You finally go to that friend, confess your fault, and ask his forgiveness. Then he says, "I freely forgive you."

How would you know you were really forgiven? How could you have an assurance that he was no longer displeased with you? Would it be by waiting for some inward impression or some outward voice or some startling light? No, it would be by simply believing your friend's word.

So it is with faith in Jesus; it rests entirely upon the merits of Christ's precious blood and knowledge that pardon has been granted, because God has said, "He that believes shall be saved." No angel has come from heaven to tell him that his sins have been blotted out and that his name is now entered in the Lamb's Book of Life, but he rests upon a testimony better than that of all the angels in heaven, even the testimony of the faithful true Witness. *He that hath received his testimony hath set to his seal that God is true* (John 3:33). We know what it is to put our name and seal on a written document. It is to ratify it and declare our determination to abide by its contents. So faith rests sweetly upon the work of Christ and upon the Word of God, and knows that peace and assurance is found there forever.

The great mistake that many make when inquiring about salvation is to refuse to come as they are to Jesus. They think they must wait for deeper conviction, more feeling, or more love for Christ before they can come to him. Therefore, they keep looking at their own hearts to find any good feeling springing up, which might form the basis of encouragement that they were becoming more fit for Christ. The Bible says, *Blessed is the people that know the joyful sound* (Psalm 89:15). That *joyful sound* comes only from Calvary. It comes from the pale lips of Jesus, quivering in death, as he says, *It is finished* (John 19:30). But the instructed sinner listens at the door of his heart to hear the joyful sound come from there. But from there it never will come. In that heart is no good thing, and no voice except that of condemnation will ever come from it.

As a scriptural illustration, the children of Israel had fiery flying serpents sent among them, the sting of which was deadly. The people were dying on the right hand and on the left. God commanded a brass serpent to be lifted up in sight of the perishing and assured them that whoever looked at it in faith would be instantly cured. A man could have been wounded and dying. His friends would take him out to within sight of the saving object; they would urge and entreat him to look at it and be saved. Instead of looking at the brass serpent, however, he kept looking at his wound. He spoke of its painfulness and the increase in bad symptoms; he bitterly lamented his miserable state. Would his looking at and talking about his malady save him? No, he would die under the very shadow of the object of salvation, not because there was no saving power in it, but because he would not do what God commanded – look at the brass serpent instead of at himself.

Jesus says, *Look unto me, and be ye saved* (Isaiah 45:22).

But you say, "I cannot go to Jesus with such a hard heart. I have too little feeling and must wait until I can get more conviction of sin."

This arises from the pride of self-righteousness in your heart. Suppose you could feel your heart growing better, and you had more feeling. Upon making this discovery, you would begin to rejoice, but what would this be but rejoicing in yourself instead of in Christ? It would only be making a savior of your feelings, your emotions, and your repentance, instead of the heaven-appointed Savior.

And this is one great reason why the religion of many of the present day who profess to believe is so erratic and unreliable. They live by feeling, and our feelings are as changeable as the whirling winds. Therefore, we cannot depend on such professors. They are either in the ecstasy of excitement or are reduced to the stupor of indifference. When they feel well, they will do well.

Their religion is not like the peaceful river, rolling calmly on day after day; but rather it is like the mountain torrent caused by heavy rain that comes foaming madly down, but is nowhere to be found in the dry season when it is most needed. It is not like the steady light of the sun, brighter and brighter to the perfect day; but it is like the glare of the lightning, which dazzles your eyes on a dark night with the sudden illumination of earth and skies and then leaves you to plod on in greater darkness than before.

True faith trusts in Jesus alone, and as he is *the same yesterday, and to day, and for ever,* its confidence is not destroyed by a change of feelings (Hebrews 13:8). On that terrible night, when "the angel of death spread his wings on the blast"[2] and breathed destruction upon the firstborn in the Egyptian families, the Israelites were saved by simply obeying the word of the Lord

---

2   George Gordon Byron, "The Destruction of Sennacherib," 1815.

and sprinkling the doorposts with blood. They did not need to barricade their doors to keep the destroyer out. It was not necessary to sit up all night, clasping the firstborn in their arms or sending up fervent prayers that he might be spared. No, if they believed the word of the Lord and did what that word required, they could go to bed and sleep calmly and sweetly under the protection of blood.

So it is with the believer in Jesus; he is under the protection of the precious blood of Christ, and he knows that his soul is safe in the keeping of infinite love. If the Israelite's faith in God's word and in the protecting power of the blood failed, he would at once be thrown into an agony of fear and doubt.

As the critical hour approached, and as he heard the first wild, despairing cry from the home of his neighbor that the destroyer had visited, he would be apt to resort to all kinds of his own devices for the protection of the loved one. If he had steady faith, however, in God's solution, then no doubts would disturb the calm restfulness of his soul.

Obedient faith finds the mountains as flat as plains.

An old writer says, "Faith will be shaken even by loose stones in the way if we look at man; if we look toward God, faith will not be rattled even with impassable mountains stretching across and obstructing our progress. 'Go forward' is the voice from heaven, and obedient faith finds the mountains as flat as plains. How strong is faith when it comes fresh from the fountain of redeeming love!"

Another old writer says, "For every look you give to your own evil heart, give fifty to Christ."

This waiting for joy and peace and love to spring up in our hearts before we believe in Jesus is as unphilosophical as it is unscriptural. We cannot produce emotions by trying to feel. Suppose I were to say, "I will now begin to feel sorry." I could not feel sorry by mere trying. But let me fix my mind upon some sorrowful subject, like my mother on her deathbed with her pale and quivering lips, giving me her dying charge. The emotion of sorrow will spring up without my trying to produce it.

If I say, "I will now begin to feel joyful," I cannot produce that emotion by any direct effort. But let me fix my mind upon some joyful fact, and at once my heart will be filled with real gladness.

So let the sinner look to Jesus as he utters the deep death groan that severs his bleeding heart. Let him believe that all this suffering, all this boundless love was for him. As one says, "He must be more or less than a man" if it does not melt him down into repentance and love. The Bible tells us that it is *faith which worketh by love* and purifies the heart (Galatians 5:6). To expect good emotions before faith in Jesus is to expect the effect before the cause.

> Let not conscience make you linger,
>   Nor of fitness fondly dream;
> All the fitness he requireth
>   Is to feel your need of him.[3]

---

[3] Joseph Hart, "Come Ye Sinners," 1759.

Chapter 6

Obscuring Clouds

The experience of all who have had the joy of being taught of Christ is that they have had more difficulty in unlearning than in learning. The prejudices produced by erroneous religious training or the opinions of men of high standing and of prominent spirituality hinder our progress. The writings of great men who are famous in the world, and a blind attachment to the church of our fathers, however far that church may be from the truth, prevent our growth. A whole bundle of preconceived notions in regard to religion, which have no foundation in the Bible, all stand in our way, as mountain barriers to the reception of the truth, for *the truth is in Jesus* (Ephesians 4:21).

It is sobering to think of the influence that prejudice will exert on the human mind on the most important subject – salvation. It spreads the darkness of midnight over our understanding, twists and distorts all our modes of reasoning and thinking, and leaves its own horrid impression upon all our conclusions. It leads men to read the Word of God not to discover truth, but to find something to sustain their favorite theories. These theories are often so absurd that the introduction of a little common sense would be enough to dispel them, as the mist is dispelled by the rising glories of the sun.

It has been said that you cannot reason a man out of a thing that he has never been reasoned into, and the only cure for this unhappy state of mind is to come to the Bible as to the foundation of truth, saying, "Lord, what I know not teach thou me."

When the voice of prejudice exclaimed, *Can there any good thing come out of Nazareth?* the happy convert who had just found the Savior, whose soul was glowing with desire for the salvation of his friend, had too much wisdom to sit down and enter into an argument about the matter. If he had done so, he probably would have lost his temper and done more harm than good; but there was holy power in the kind reply, *Come and see* (John 1:46).

There is the greatest difference among men as to the reception of gospel truth. Some receive the truth the first time they hear it. With the rapidity of lightning, conviction of their lost state flashes upon their minds, and they immediately go to Jesus for pardon. They remember the day and the hour when they were converted. Most of the conversions recorded in the New Testament are of this character.

But with many who are truly the Lord's children, it is quite different. The light of the gospel breaks upon their minds gradually, as the dawning of the day. They cannot tell of sudden terrors, appalling alarms, or powerful convictions, hurrying them on to the verge of despair and shaking their souls over the fiery gulf. One person said, "The Lord awoke me as the mother awakes her babe – with a kiss."

Neither can such persons tell of great exhilaration and ecstatic joys in their conversion. That the truth as it is in Jesus in its celestial grandeur has settled upon their souls, there can be no doubt. They know that Christ is unspeakably precious to their souls, and there is no hesitation in the tone with which they say, *One thing I know, that, whereas I was blind, I now see* (John 9:25). However, they cannot fix the very day when this great change took place. They often write bitter things against themselves because of this and fear that they have never been converted at all. But let such persons remember that to be *in Christ* is the essential thing; the way in which we have reached that place of safety is of little concern.

> *To be in Christ is the essential thing; the way in which we have reached that place of safety is of little concern.*

When the floodgates of heaven were opened in Noah's time, and a wild deluge was about to sweep the globe of its guilty inhabitants, to be *in* the ark was to be safe, whether the ark had been reached by a few rapid bounds or by slow and halting steps. So to be able to say, *I found him whom my soul loveth* (Song of Solomon 3:4) is of vastly more importance than to be able to relate an experience with a thrilling succession of feelings, and with dates as correct as the revolutions of the earth.

One great reason many are kept from accepting salvation by faith in Jesus is because of preconceived and erroneous opinions as to what religion truly is. They have decided what they must do and how they must feel if they are ever to become Christians. They have marked out a process in their minds through which they think they must go, a process composed of weeks or months of gloom and terror of soul, of bitter tears and agonizing prayers, followed by a sudden gush of joy. They presume the whole process is as distinctly marked as the various stages of an intermittent fever. They think that when all these emotions have been experienced, God will change his feelings toward them, and his anger will be turned away from them. They believe he will forgive their past offenses and love them freely after considering the great change that has taken place in them.

But tell them:

- that this attempt to change God and become more acceptable to him by their own efforts is not only foolishness but also wickedness;

- that they are repudiating God's plan of saving them and daring to substitute one of their own;

- that no change needs to be effected in God, as he has already so loved them as to give his Son to die for them; and

- that there is now absolutely nothing between them and pardon and justification except

> to believe in the perfect satisfaction which
> Jesus has made to a broken and insulted law.

Tell them all this, and you dismantle the notions and feelings that have been strengthened by the culture and compliance of years.

The state of mind described is illustrated by the case of Naaman the Syrian (2 Kings 5). This man had a dangerous and loathsome disease, which cast a dark shadow over his life. The good news reached his ears that a man of God lived in the land of Israel who could cure him; he immediately started upon his journey, surrounded with all that pomp and grandeur which his wealth enabled him to command. As he drew near to the residence of the man of God, he determined in his own mind the whole method of his cure. He already imagined how the prophet would hasten to meet him and move his hand over the diseased place. He thought the prophet would lift up his eyes to heaven and invoke the Almighty, and his whole frame would thrill under the consciousness of a perfect cure.

This was Naaman's plan, but it was not God's. The simple message was sent to him: *Go and wash in Jordan seven times, . . . and thou shalt be clean* (2 Kings 5:10). What a severe blow to the man's preconceived notions! The scowl of displeasure was on his brow, and indignation was in his heart, because God did not carry out Naaman's plan. God's way for a cure was too simple and too humbling to his pride. But at last, through the persuasions of his servants, he did what the Lord commanded, and at once he was made whole.

So, my dear reader, cast away your own notions

and prejudices. Cast from you with a noble scorn the self-righteous pride that would lead you to question the wisdom of God's way of saving you, and this hour salvation shall come to your heart.

Consider that poor diseased woman in the days of our Lord, pressing her way through the crowd so she may touch the hem of his garment. She was pale, weak, and helpless in herself. The crowd, surging and swaying, sometimes carried her far from Jesus, the object of her hope. But she did not give up. She did not say, "What can such a poor, weak invalid as I am do?" She did not sit down and philosophize about what the likelihood was of a mere touch of the hem of the Lord's garment doing her any good. She pressed her way forward, and at last her trembling hand touched his garment. At once her bent and shriveled form straightened into health and vigor. Our Lord instantly looked around and inquired who had touched him. There were many crowding and pressing upon him, but he knew that one believing soul in particular had touched him with the hand of faith. He felt that healing power had gone forth from him to some believing heart.

That blessed Savior is also near you while you read these lines. You don't need to ascend to the heights to bring him down or descend into the depths to bring him up. You don't need to go to the uttermost ends of the earth to pursue him; you don't need to wait to find him at lengthy meetings or repentant seats, though many

> *Cast from you the self-righteous pride that would lead you to question God's way of saving you.*

have found him there. He is near you at this moment, even in your heart if you only believe his Word. There is only the veil of unbelief between you and him at this moment; let that be torn away, and the peace of heaven will flood your heart as you cry, *My Lord and my God* (John 20:28).

It often happens that after the plan of salvation has been presented in the plainest way, we are met by the assertion: "I cannot believe." Now, this is an assertion, which plainly contradicts your Maker to his face. The Lord who made you must know what you can and what you cannot do. The very fact that he commands you to believe, and threatens you with eternal punishment for not believing is the greatest evidence that you can do it.

Jesus says, *Ye will not come to me, that ye might have life* (John 5:40). Yet, you have the boldness to say to that Savior, "I cannot come unto thee."

Suppose, for example, that a man has insulted his best friend, and when urged to go and confess his fault and ask his friend's forgiveness, he says, "I cannot do it." What does he mean by that *cannot*? Does he mean that his limbs have become paralyzed, so that he cannot go to his friend's house? No. Does he mean that he has lost the power of speech, so that he cannot ask the injured man's forgiveness? No. The meaning of his *cannot* is that he has such an obstinate, bad temper that he will not do it. The perverse pride of his heart is such that he will not do what the voice of God above him and the voice of conscience within him declare to be his imperative duty.

It is so with the sinner. He goes about with a great

deal of zeal to establish a righteousness for himself, but he will not submit himself to the righteousness of Christ. He thinks he is very humble, very brokenhearted and contrite; he declares his willingness to do anything required of him. Ask him to stand up in public and express his desire for the prayers of God's people, and he will promptly do it. Ask him to attend a confirmation meeting, and he will do that. Ask him to go home and pray and read his Bible, and his compliance is prompt. But there is one thing he will not do: he will not do the very first thing that his God requires of him – believe in Jesus. He says he has repented of sin and proclaims a readiness to give up every sin, but the very first sin the Spirit points out, he refuses to abandon – the sin of unbelief.

He is like a man who has a broken limb. The physician is called in, and the man claims to be willing to let his medical attendant handle the limb in whatever way may be necessary. The hand of skill passes along the limb, pressing here and there, until it rests upon the injured part. Then the patient flinches and exclaims, "Ah, Doctor, you must not touch there!"

"Yes, but," says the doctor, "that is the very place that needs to be touched, and if you will not let me touch that, there is no use of my staying here."

So, sinner, the Spirit of God pours a whole flood of light on the sin of unbelief and points that out as the murderer of your soul. You not only refuse to give it up, but you also speak as if you could not give it up, and your God has laid you under the absolute necessity of calling him a liar. Don't you see there is an immense depth of pride in your heart that is keeping you from Jesus? If you are willing to be saved, the Savior is willing; what then is to hinder the lost from being found? No more precious blood was shed for John, or for Peter, or for Paul than has been shed for you. If ever you are saved at all, you must be saved as they were – by the application of that blood to your own soul by faith. There is no reason on God's part why you should not this moment be saved. Any barriers that remain are of your own building and supporting. Throw open the door of your heart, and invite the blessed Lord to come in.

There is no reason on God's part why you should be saved. Any barriers that remain are of your own building.

> Ye ransomed of Jesus,
> > Come sing of His love!
> He stooped down to raise us
> > To mansions above:
> Jehovah on Him our transgressions did lay;
> > He bore the dread burden, and bore it away.[4]

---

4   John Guthrie, "The Love of Jesus," *Sacred Lyrics: Hymns, Original, and Translated from the German* (London: James Nisbet & Co., 1869), 7.

Chapter 7

Mighty to Save

Souls fleeing from the wrath to come often need great encouragement. Satan will do what he can to keep a man from becoming a Christian, but if he cannot succeed in this, he will try to make him as miserable a Christian as possible by doubts and fears. This Enemy of souls first tries to lull souls to sleep in an overconfident security. By false representations of the general mercy of God, by perverted views of the nature of sin, and by preaching from the old, popular, and pleasing text, *Ye shall not surely die* (Genesis 3:4), he will try to keep all thoughts of the coming wrath from disturbing your soul.

But, if he cannot succeed in this, and his hellish logic cannot keep the soul from concern about its state before God, then the Father of Lies will try to persuade the sinner that there is no salvation for him. Therefore, you will see the same man rush from the extreme of assurance to that of despair in the course of a few hours. Formerly he could not be made to fear, but now he cannot be made to hope. I'd like to address him in the following remarks.

Such persons are as much in the service of the devil in their present state of mind as they ever were. They may go to the house of God, attend confirmation meetings, converse with religious people freely, and appear to be more religious than they ever were, but they still believe Satan's lie in opposition to God's truth. They are entrenched in unbelief and refuse to trust the imperishable Word of the God of truth, casting the precious promises back in the face of the Eternal.

Two great truths stand out so plain on the pages of the Bible that he who strives may read them. The one is that if any sinner is ever saved, God deserves all the glory; the other is that if any sinner is ever lost, the sinner gets all the blame. God has joined these two truths together, and let no man dare to separate them. We may talk about God's sovereignty and man's free will, and about liberty and necessity until we and our hearers become lost in the thick metaphysical fog of our own making. But thank God, when we emerge from the thick darkness of our own creating, we see these two truths in the Word of Life shining out gloriously – lights in a dark place to which we should take heed.

God has taken infinite pains to convince the sinner that he has no pleasure in the sinner's death.

God has taken infinite pains to convince the sinner that he has no pleasure in the sinner's death. He casts the whole responsibility of his soul's eternal state upon that person. To set this matter forever at rest and shut the mouth of unbelief, the eternal God comes before the assembled world of his own guilty creatures in infinite humility. He swears by his own Being not only that he has no pleasure in the death of a sinner but that he also has a contrary pleasure – a pleasure in his conversion. Now, it is said that among men *an oath for confirmation is to them an end of all strife* (Hebrews 6:16), but it seems that between the sinner and God, it is not the end of all strife. It seems that after refusing to believe the Word of God, the sinner will go on to doubt his very oath! Oh, how deep and damning is the sin of unbelief!

The doctrine that God honestly and earnestly desires the salvation of the sinner is taught everywhere in the Bible and in the strongest terms. First Timothy 2:3-4 says, *For this is good and acceptable in the sight of God our Saviour; who will have all men to be saved, and to come unto the knowledge of the truth.* Second Peter 3:9 tells us that God is *not willing that any should perish, but that all should come to repentance.* Many other passages might be quoted to show how earnestly God longs for the salvation of the greatest sinner, and that when the sinner perishes, it is not because there is no love for him in the heart of God. It is not because the blood of Jesus has not been shed for him, and it is not because that blood, so efficacious to save others, has no power to save him. It is simply because he persistently refuses to be saved by God's appointed method – faith in the death and righteousness of the Lord Jesus.

If God is a holy God, as is universally acknowledged, then he must desire to see all men holy. And, as an evidence of this, when a little of God's own Spirit takes possession of any man, from that moment he begins intensely to long and pray for the salvation of all. Now, if a very little of God's Spirit in the heart of a Christian makes him desire the salvation of all men, does the Spirit itself only desire the salvation of a few? Ask any good man when the spirit of prayer is imparted to him, how many perishing sinners he desires to be saved, and he will at once exclaim, "Oh, all that my Savior knows."

Now, that desire did not come naturally, neither did it come from the Prince of Darkness, but it is in his possession because he has been made a *[partaker] of the divine nature,* because *the mind of Christ* is in him (2 Peter 1:4; 1 Corinthians 2:16). In short, the fervent longing of the believer for the salvation of the world, which shows itself in tears, prayers, and persevering efforts, is but the echo of the voice that comes from the eternal throne. *As I live, . . . I have no pleasure in the death of him that dieth, saith the Lord GOD: wherefore turn yourselves, and live* (Ezekiel 18:3, 32).

Consider the unquestionable proof that these were God's feelings toward a perishing world: when he gave his beloved Son, he sent a company of holy angels to announce the errand on which he came – not as a Savior for a few but for all. *Fear not: for, behold, I bring you good tidings of great joy, which shall be to all people* (Luke 2:10). Now, if Jesus did not die for all, if salvation is not free to all, then the gospel could not be glad tidings to any of us.

Suppose that a number of persons are confined in prison under the sentence of death. One night the door of their cell is thrown open, and a messenger from the governor enters, saying, "Cheer up, my friends, I have good news for you." They would all expect to hear something that would make them happy. Every eye is fixed on the face of the messenger, and their interest is intense, when he breaks the deep silence once more by saying, "There is pardon and deliverance for *some* of you."

This would not really be good news to any of them; it would not really make any of them happy. Since they could not know who the favored ones were, those words would cast them back into greater suspense and anxiety than before. But if a free pardon is offered to all without exception, it can truly be called good news whether it is received or not. Some might be too proud to accept it, and others might think they could save themselves in some other way than by accepting an offer of free grace. Nevertheless, the message itself was glad tidings and was for all the condemned.

If a free pardon is offered to all without exception, it can truly be called good news whether it is received or not.

Our precious Redeemer must have known what the nature of his mission would be and whether the work that he undertook was for the whole race or only for part of it. And, accordingly, his account of it is: *God so loved the world, that he gave his only begotten Son, that whosoever believeth in him should not perish, but have everlasting life* (John 3:16). Sinner, there are two words here that refer to you, however great your sins may have been. God loved *the world;* you are one of the world. Therefore, God so loved *you* as to give his

Son to die for you. The word *whosoever* also includes you. It includes the whole world who will believe in him whose blood cleanses from *all* sin.

Indeed, had the death of our Lord Jesus not been for all, and had his love not gone out equally to all, it could not be said of him that he kept the law, that he magnified the law, and that he made it honorable. The law required him not only to love God with all his soul, but also to love *his neighbor as himself*. In taking our nature upon himself, he became the neighbor of every man according to his own definition of *neighbor* as given in the parable of the good Samaritan. Had his love been only a partial love, had it taken in only one portion of the race and rejected the other, he would not have been a perfect Savior.

But, as facts sometimes impact the mind more forcibly than arguments, permit me to turn your attention to a few facts that show the Lord Jesus as mighty to save the vilest of transgressors. One day the Lord visited Capernaum; he was invited to dinner at the house of a Pharisee. While he sat at the table, a woman, whose past life had been stained by sins of the deepest dye, came into the room. She had doubtless been listening to his soul-searching preaching, which had convicted her of her lost condition and made all of her past life pass in terrible review before her frightened spirit. She washed our Lord's feet with her tears of repentance and wiped them with her hair. To show the full extent of her grateful heart, she anointed him with a very costly oil.

The Pharisee was dreadfully shocked at such things being allowed in his house, and his proud heart swelled with indignation as he said within himself, *This man, if he were a prophet, would have known who and what manner of woman this is that toucheth him: for she is a sinner* (Luke 7:39). Poor, spiritually blind mortal! The blessed Redeemer knew well who she was and her past life, but he also knew the deep repentance and the strong faith which filled her heart. Turning to her, after a keen rebuke to the Pharisee, he said, *Thy faith hath saved thee* (Luke 7:50).

But we have a still more notable case. Jesus is on the cross in the midst of mortal agonies. The hour of darkness has now come, and the curse due to guilty sinners is fallen upon his holy head. Around him a perfect tempest of passion is raging, and the very men for whose guilt he is suffering are blaspheming him with a thousand tongues. And, worse than all the pains that rack his body, worse than the ravings of blasphemy at the foot of the cross, the light of his Father's smiles in which he had rejoiced from all eternity are now withdrawn. The dismal gloom which falls upon the earth is only a faint image of the darkness that covers his holy mind, as he exclaims, *My God, my God, why hast thou forsaken me?* (Matthew 27:46).

Yet, even in that terrible hour, he does not forget to labor for the souls of the perishing. He doubtless preaches the kingdom of God to the two fellow sufferers, and one of them receives the truth and is saved. He was suffering punishment as a thief who had violated the laws of both God and man, but his past sins formed no barrier to Christ receiving him. He had no good works to present for which he could claim acceptance with God. But blessed be God, they were not needed! He found the blood of Jesus a sufficient plea for his justification, and Jesus' righteousness an ample covering for his naked soul.

He was a bad man who had been so hardened in sin that even his fellow man could endure him no longer. They were determined to rid the earth of his vile presence by pushing him before the judgment bar of God. In the last hour of his wasted life, however, he believed in Jesus, and in that moment his past guilt was all forgiven, and the promise of eternal life fell from the lips of Jesus upon his dying ear. Oh sinner, why stay away one hour longer from such a Savior who will in no wise cast out any that come to him?

We have thus seen what were the terms upon which Jesus received sinners in the days of his humanity, but he is no longer on earth, and the question occurs – Is he still the same? We are so likely to change ourselves and are surrounded with so many changes that we are apt to suspect a change in the Friend of sinners. But the Word of God assures us that he is *the same yesterday, and to day, and for ever* (Hebrews 13:8), and as a proof of it, we see him receiving the chief of sinners after his glorious ascension.

Shortly after Jesus went to his throne in glory, a young man of advanced education and of great intellect launched a course of opposition to the Lord's cause. Possessed of great energy of character and a determined spirit that never did anything halfheartedly, he persecuted the followers of Jesus to death, and to use his own words, was *exceedingly mad against them* (Acts 26:11).

As he went on in his career of blasphemy and blood, the eye of the Savior looked down upon him, a witness of all the dark passions that filled his heart.

And did that eye flash with the fires of wrath? Did a red thunderbolt leap from the hands of the Lord to dash this rebel wretch to pieces? No, the eye that once swam in tears for him still pitied him. The hand that was once nailed to the cross for him graciously stretched out to pluck him from destruction. His blasphemies were turned into prayers; his hatred of Christ and his people turned into love. Thirty years later, remembering the whole scene on the road to Damascus, he says, *This is a faithful saying, and worthy of all acceptation, that Christ Jesus came into the world to save sinners; of whom I am chief* (1 Timothy 1:15).

Reader, will you now believe? I have no way of knowing how great a sinner you have been, but in the name of Jesus, I declare you are welcome to a Savior who is *mighty to save* (Isaiah 63:1). The terms of Solomon's pardon to Adonijah were: *If he will shew himself a worthy man* (1 Kings 1:52). But Christ's offer of pardon is not burdened with *if.* He receives the unworthy who believe in him, and through his worthiness makes them worthy. His name is Jesus because he saves from sin. An old writer says, "There is majesty in the name *God.* There is independent being in the name *Jehovah.* There is unction in the name *Christ.* There is friendship in the word *Immanuel.* There is help in the name *Advocate.* But there is salvation only in the name *Jesus.*"

Chapter 8

Peace with God

The most valuable blessing that man can enjoy on earth is peace with God. When the blessed Redeemer was about to bid his disciples farewell, and they stood around him in speechless sorrow, peace was the gift that he granted them as his parting legacy. He was Lord of all and owned the whole universe from which to choose a gift for them in that hour of parting tenderness. The gift which he chose as the most precious for them in their hour of need was peace with God. *Peace I leave with you, my peace I give unto you: not as the world giveth, give I unto you* (John 14:27).

Notice that the Savior did not say that he would give the believer *a* peace. The world can do that. The false hope that causes shame can do that. But he promised to give his own peace – the same untroubled calm that dwelt in his inmost heart from all eternity.

Before you could make an animal happy with man's happiness, you would have to give it man's nature, and before the soul can be happy with God's peace, it must first become a partaker of God's nature. This occurs when the soul believes in Jesus and casts itself unreservedly upon his promises. *Whereby are given unto us exceeding great and precious promises: that by these [we] might be partakers of the divine nature* (2 Peter 1:4). Man lost his happiness when he lost the image of God upon his soul, and he can never be happy until that image is restored. No outward surrounding can make him happy while he has no peace with God.

Why was Adam unhappy after he became a sinner? He was still in Paradise with all its scenes of surpassing loveliness. The heavens were as bright above him and the earth as beautiful around him as before, and yet he trembled with guilty terror and sought to hide himself from the presence of his God. The reason is that sin had entered his soul, and instead of peace, there was misery and internal discord. *There is no peace, saith my God, to the wicked* (Isaiah 57:21).

You might place a sinner in a palace and ransack the four quarters of the globe to find objects for his pleasures. The voices of applauding thousands might shout his praise. A crowd of flatterers might bow at his nod, but sin reigning in his heart would convert everything into the misery of hell. Sin would make his sweetest music as harsh and discordant as the groans of the damned. His soul would convulse as the gasping of those in the burning lake and send out from his heart the cry, *All is vanity and vexation of spirit* (Ecclesiastes 1:14).

Almost every good thing in this world has its

counterfeit, and so it is with peace with God. The prophet Jeremiah tells of some in his day who cried, *Peace, peace; when there [was] no peace* (Jeremiah 6:14).

The prophet wept bitterly over their lost condition, but they had not one tear to shed for themselves. He saw the extent of their tremendous peril, but no fear disturbed their deadly stupor. Such persons fondly suppose that all is right with them, while all is wrong. They are spiritually bankrupt, while they think themselves *rich, and increased in goods* (Revelation 3:17).

Almost every good thing in this world has its counterfeit, and so it is with peace with God.

Perhaps there was a time when deep conviction of sin shook their souls to their very center. The terrors of the Lord and the powers of the world to come made them afraid. Their feelings were aroused to the highest pitch of human endurance. They longed for peace and comfort to come to them from somewhere. Now, in the very nature of things, the sinner will not remain in this state for long. If he does not immediately go to Jesus and receive true peace, he will return to a callous indifference on the subject of religion or settle for some false hope.

It is a law of all nature that whatever is violent cannot endure. When we see a violent storm, we know that it will not last long. The violent disease soon exhausts itself or the patient. The grief that is furious and clamorous over the grave of a friend seldom lasts long. So, when the mind is deeply moved to sorrow and alarm on the subject of religion, this philosophy of the mind anticipates a reaction – that a calm will ensue. The great danger is that unless the mind is faithfully dealt with, this calm will be mistaken for the peace of God.

That this is the case with thousands of professing Christians is evident from the fact that they can give no scriptural and intelligent reason for the hope that is in them. They felt very bad, and after a time they felt better; this is about the sum total of their religious experience. As to how a just and holy God can forgive them without dishonoring his law and compromising his truth, they can give no scriptural account. If they attempt to direct an anxious sinner to be saved, they exhibit the spectacle of the blind leading the blind.

Their religion is founded upon feelings, not principles; it soon settles into a heartless form. Should the truth of God ever startle their slumbering souls into alarm that all is not right with them, they immediately find comfort by falling back on their religious experience and living in the remote past. There is no congregation so hard to be reached by divine truth as those who have thus pillowed their head upon a false peace. The pastor may preach the most faithful and powerful discourses with a heart filled with intense compassion for the perishing. He may expose the danger of self-deceivers with a clearness and fidelity that will sometimes alarm the true saints of God. As an old writer says, "It is hard to drive the dogs out without making the children cry," but the deluded soul clutches the huge falsehood with which it is descending to destruction with a tighter grasp.

Oh, dear reader, carefully look to the foundation of your peace. If you make a mistake in your daily business, it may be corrected and no great harm done. If, in the building of a house, the construction of a machine, or the solving of a difficult problem you make a mistake, the work may be done over and all be made right; but if you die wrong, it is an eternal mistake! There is no coming back from the land of despair to correct mistakes made with reference to salvation. When the day of grace has ended, every stream of mercy dried up, and the light of hope quenched in darkness, then the insulted justice will inflict avenging strokes upon the soul, and eternity will be filled with the doleful lamentation, "The harvest is past, the summer is ended, and I am not saved."

This peace is the only real support in the midst of the trials and sorrows of life. Earth has no ill for which Jesus doesn't have a cure. The heart knows its own bitterness, and we are sometimes called to pass through afflictions in which the most tender human sympathy can do us no good. Human comforters may offer temporary relief like a stupefying opiate given to the pain-racked sufferer, but Jesus can give a peace lasting for eternity.

Earth has no ill for which Jesus doesn't have a cure.

Many are the remedies proposed for the sorrows of life. One person who is under the deep afflictions from his circumstances frets, murmurs, complains, and makes himself and all those around him miserable by pouring out his grievances. Another person may continue under his trials with a hardened indifference, submit to what he calls fate, and sullenly declare that he must bear what he cannot control. Finding comfort in these ways may be said like Job's friends: *Miserable comforters are ye all* (Job 16:2).

When trouble comes to the believer, he has a much different comfort. He may be placed in the most trying circumstances, and every door of outward enjoyment may be shut, but then Jesus speaks to his soul, and in his own mild accents of love, says, *Peace be unto you* (John 20:21). Consider Paul and Silas in a gloomy prison (Acts 16:16-40). Their persecutors had scourged them until blood trickled down on the floor of their cell; their feet were held fast in the stocks. Locked up in that darkness and gloom, their state of mind could have been one of unmingled misery. But in their hearts, the imperishable principle of peace with God reigned; they were so happy that they broke out into a song of such enthusiastic joy that the old prison walls echoed with the very melody of heaven.

The man who has this peace can meet earthly trials not only calmly and undauntedly but also rejoicingly for the experience of the hand of his heavenly Father. A shower of afflictions may fall upon him like the stones upon the head of the dying Stephen; yet like him, he can see the heavens opened and the face of his Lord beaming with a smile of approval. Like the three Hebrews in Babylon, he may be cast into the fiery furnace; but like them, One walks with him who is like the Son of God. Like Peter, Satan may desire to have him so that he may sift him as wheat; but like him, he can hear his Lord say, *I have prayed for thee, that thy faith fail not* (Luke 22:32). His frail bark may be launched upon a turbulent sea of troubles, but across the billows he sees Jesus coming to comfort him in the dark night of his sorrow. "With Christ in the vessel," he says, "I smile at the storm."[5]

Dear reader, to convince you that this is not empty theory or a mere flourish of rhetoric, come with me on one of my pastoral visits. We will enter this humble dwelling, and as we enter the sickroom, we tread softly for we are on holy ground. Angels are there, and the Lord of angels is there. Upon the bed lies a kind Christian wife and mother who is about to close her eyes on earthly objects.

By the bedside stands her husband in deep distress, bidding her farewell as she sinks into the cold river of death. There, too, are the little children, soon to be motherless, listening to her parting words and planting their last kiss on those cold lips that taught them to say, "Our Father who art in heaven." She hugs her baby to her loving heart, which is already struck with the chill of death, and lifting her eyes to heaven, she offers her last prayer. And then with a countenance beaming with peace, she says, "My blessed Savior has come; I hear him say, 'I have loved thee with an everlasting love; I have graven thee upon the palms of my hands'" (Jeremiah 31:3; Isaiah 49:16). She speaks to her weeping friends about a bright world where parting is unknown, where death never shows its ghastly face, and where all that is pure becomes permanent.

In this way peace with God gives complete victory over death. When his legs were consumed by the fire,

---

[5] John Newton, "Begone Unbelief," 1779.

John Lambert, who was burned to death for Christ's sake in Smithfield, lifted up his hand, his fingers blazing like torches, and cried with his last breath, "None but Christ! None but Christ!"

That great and good man Samuel Rutherford said to some ministers who came to see him on his deathbed, "Brethren, do all for Christ: pray for Christ, preach for Christ, feed the flock for Christ, visit the sick for Christ, do all for Christ."

The dying words of John Knox were, "Come, Lord Jesus; sweet Jesus, into thy hands I commend my spirit."

The biographer of John Eliot, the missionary among the Indians, tells us that on his deathbed "he was full of peace, of hope, of a calm and full trust in Jesus; nothing could shake his humility, like a guardian angel, ever hovered around his heart and kept it in safety." Reader, prepare to meet thy God. Get the peace that does not make you ashamed by faith in Jesus, and death will be great gain to you.

> Is that a death-bed where a Christian lies?—
> Yes! but not his—'tis Death itself there dies.[6]

---

[6] Samuel Taylor Coleridge, "On His Baptismal Birthday," 1833.

Chapter 9

The Thirsty Invited

Ho, every one that thirsteth, come ye to the waters, and he that hath no money; come ye, buy, and eat; yea, come, buy wine and milk without money and without price. (Isaiah 55:1)

Dear reader, if you were traveling along a public highway and heard a loud "Ho!" uttered behind you, three questions would naturally occur to you. First, who is speaking? Secondly, to whom is he speaking? And thirdly, what did he say? Now, we are traveling to eternity, and we have listened to the solemn call contained in the above text. Let me direct your attention to these three questions.

Who is speaking? The great God of heaven and earth is the One who is addressing us. The God who guides the planets in their courses and regulates the wanderings of the flaming comet speaks to us. He who sustains all life, from the worm that crawls beneath our feet to the angel who rolls his eternal song through the courts of heaven, speaks to us. He whose almighty voice is heard both in the sighing of a breeze and in the thunder that rolls in terrific majesty across the heavens condescends to speak to guilty sinners like us. Oh, let us listen with profound awe, for his very forgiveness is to be feared.

When we open the pages of the Bible or go to the house of God, we are apt to feel as if we only hear man speak to us. The result is that we sit in judgment upon the Word instead of permitting the Word to sit in judgment upon us.

We are so accustomed to hearing and handling the Word of God that we fail to realize that it truly is God speaking to us.

If we had stood on the banks of the Jordan on the occasion of our Lord's baptism and heard the voice of God directly addressing us from the heavens, we think that we would have felt it uniquely solemn. If, while sitting in our own home, we were to see a hand move before us and write a direct personal appeal on the wall, we think we could never forget it. But in reality there is nothing more solemn in God's speaking to us in an audible voice from heaven or in God writing a message upon the wall than there is in God writing it in his Word and causing the divine Spirit to point at our hearts and say, *Thou art the man* (2 Samuel 12:7).

But the fact remains that we are so accustomed to hearing and handling the Word of God from our youth that we fail to realize that it truly is God speaking to us. This tendency to become hardened and indifferent under the very abundance of our religious privileges is a sad sign of the deep depravity of our hearts. A stranger visiting Niagara Falls for the first time is thrilled with awe and trembles at the sound of nature's most majestic voice as *deep calleth unto deep* (Psalm 42:7), but the people who have lived beside the mighty waterfall all their days are apt to regard it with indifference and scarcely heed the tones of its powerful voice.

Likewise, we have seen many an outcast wanderer, who has not entered the house of God for many years, fall down in brokenhearted remorse after the first sermon he hears, while gospel-hardened sinners sit with utter carelessness as they hear the rebukes of the Almighty. That Holy Bible in your home is a tremendous visitor. From week to week, the whole year long, it utters God's voice to you. Its presence in your household is one of the most sacred resources of your life. By it you are to be judged on the last day, and above the ashes of a consumed world, that voice you now have little regard for will pronounce your unchangeable doom.

We come to the next question: To whom is he speaking? God addresses the whole world here, and yet he is not speaking to the inhabitants of the world collectively, but individually. He is speaking to us one by one as we pass before him, in the words, *Ho, every one.* There is a beautiful appropriateness in this, when we remember that men are to be judged individually. It was so when man first sinned. Adam was first called up and judged, then Eve, and then Satan. And in the great day of final accounting, every man is to receive according to the deeds done in his body, and all will find their minutest affairs investigated, as if they alone had occupied the undivided attention of the judge.

If men are to get spiritual profit from the preaching of the gospel, it is when they realize that the Word is a personal appeal to them. As long as the sinner can hide in the multitude and talk about how the preacher spoke to the people, as if it did not concern him, the Word is more an aroma of death than of life to his soul. But when the pulpit becomes a judgment seat to him, and when his long-forgotten sins are brought up in review, the preaching becomes personal to him. When he is made to forget others around him due to his own individual responsibility to God, and he is prepared to take the whole guilt of his sins upon himself and thus justify God and condemn himself, he becomes honest with himself and God. When he no longer wishes to have lighthearted ideas prophesied to him, but places himself under the most searching and faithful ministry he can find, he will open his heart to the rebukes of the Lord who says, *Search me, O God, and know my heart: try me, and know my thoughts: and see if there be any wicked way in me* (Psalm 139:23-24). Then, and not until then, is the soul in a state to give a hearty welcome to Christ's proclamation of love, that love which thrills the heart with all the power of a personal appeal: *To you is the word of this salvation sent* (Acts 13:26).

God is speaking to the world in Isaiah 55:1 as at a distance from him. How do I know this? I know it by the use of the word *Ho*. We never cry "Ho!" to someone who is standing near us, but to those who are at a distance and whose attention we wish to secure. This distance of the sinner from his God is not a local or a geographical one. In that sense he is always near God. His future judge is by his bed, along his path, and spies out all his ways. With company or alone, when plunging into the mad scenes of amusement or devoured by the iron tooth of remorse in secret, that eye that darts through creation at a glance is fixed upon him. This thought troubles him and destroys much of the pleasure from his lips. Wretched man! He cannot even flee from himself, much less from his God. The sinner's distance from his God is a spiritual one.

In that state of mind the sinner makes a desperate effort to forget God, and though surrounded by God, spared by his grace, and fed by his providence, God is not in all his thoughts. In that state of mind, he can live as a practical atheist in a world full of God.

The sinner's distance from his God is a spiritual one.

He forms plans of happiness, but God is not in any of them. He enters upon projects that will not resemble a bit of God's holy eye, and nothing makes him more uneasy than any allusion to the fact that the Holy One is near. Therefore, he speaks a great deal about the order of nature, the works of nature, and the laws of nature; he has exalted a certain deity called chance over the world. Poor man, he is living in the "far country," self-exiled from all that can make life worth possessing and yet glorying in his shame.

God is speaking to you now. Today is his acceptable time to speak words of salvation to you. Don't refuse to listen to him now or dare to bid the Almighty to wait for your convenience. We know he waits to be gracious, but tomorrow may be too late forever! At any moment, life's pendulum may cease its rhythmic swing and stand still; the lamp of life may flicker, go out, and leave you to fill eternity with the bitter lamentation, "The harvest is past, the summer is ended, and I am not saved."

A late writer, when making an appeal to sinners, used the following illustration:

On a part of the British coast where prominent cliffs from three to five hundred feet in height overhang the ocean, some individuals obtain a solitary livelihood by collecting the eggs of rock birds and gathering samphire, a succulent, salt-tolerant plant, during a certain season of the year. To pursue these is a hazardous calling: The man drives an iron crowbar securely into the ground about a yard from the edge of the precipice. To that crowbar, he fastens a rope, which he then grips. He slides gently over the cliff and lowers himself until he reaches the ledges and crags, where he expects to find the objects of his pursuit.

To reach these places is often a difficult task, and when they fall within the perpendicular, the adventurer must swing in the air until, by an adept movement, he can balance himself in a way to reach the spot on which he wishes to descend. A specially made basket is strapped between his shoulders and carries the fruit of his labor. When he has filled the basket or failed in the attempt, he ascends, hand over hand, to the summit.

On one occasion, a man who was thus employed

gained a narrow ledge of rock, which was overhung by a higher portion of the cliff, and secured his footing, but let go of the rope. He at once perceived his peril. No one could come to his rescue or even hear his cries. The fearful alternative immediately flashed on his mind – it was, being starved to death or dashed to pieces four hundred feet below. On turning around, he saw the rope he had released, but it was far away. As it swung back and forth, its long arc testified to the mighty efforts he had used to reach the deplorable predicament in which he stood. He looked at the rope in agony. He had gazed only a little while, when he noticed that every movement was shorter than the one preceding it, so each time it came near, it was gradually reaching a point of rest; it was a little farther off than it had been the time before. He briefly reasoned: "That rope is my only chance of life; in a little while it will be forever beyond my reach; it is nearer now than it will ever be again; I can only die, so here goes!" As he said this, he sprang from the cliff as the rope was approaching, caught it in his grasp, and went home rejoicing.

In the case of this man, every moment's delay was making his chance more hopeless. As he gazed upon that rope, he knew it was nearer to him at that time than it ever would be again. He therefore took the only wise course, and immediately leaped for the rope.

Dear reader, you stand on the brink of the eternal world, and if you are not in Christ, your peril is extreme. Above you is a God whose law you have broken, whose Son you have insulted, and whose dread curse you have braved. Beneath you is the pit of woe, made ripe for devouring vengeance by your rejection of Christ, that opens to receive your soul. Behind you is nothing but a moral waste, strewn with the wreck of abused privileges, neglected Sabbaths, despised prayers and counsels of pious parents and heaven-sent ministers, and dark traces of your sins. There is not a moment to be lost. The Lord Jesus lets down the rope of salvation within your reach. The voice of your God in heaven urges you to grasp it now, or it may be forever too late! Angels pause on the wing of love to see what you will do; all heaven is interested in the result; all hell is moved for your destruction. This moment, while your eye is upon these lines, cast yourself in simple trust upon the merits of that Savior, who *save[s] them to the uttermost that come unto God by him* (Hebrews 7:25).

We come now to the third question: What did he say? The whole world is invited to come and accept salvation under the symbol of water. This is a symbol which is very frequently used in the Scriptures with beautiful appropriateness. On *that great day of the feast, Jesus stood and cried, saying, If any man thirst, let him come unto me, and drink* (John 7:37). Water is essential to our existence and is therefore appropriately used as a sign of the salvation that is in Christ. If our fountains of water failed for even a few days, or if God withheld for a little time the showers that water the earth, one wild cry of misery would go up from the earth's population. If God continued to cut off our supplies of water, our world would soon become one vast tomb.

So, salvation through the death of Jesus is essential to the life of the soul. Many think that human nature is not so utterly depraved that it cannot restore itself; they believe there is a little spark of holiness left, a little regenerating principle that only needs to be nurtured and cherished to make man all that his God can reasonably require him to be. This development theory – the idea that man has a little spiritual capital to start with, which if used properly, will make him rich towards God – is one that is exceedingly popular in the present day. It builds up the pride of human nature and allows man to glory in self.

But it is as false as it is dangerous. The Lord says, *Except ye eat the flesh of the Son of man, and drink his blood, ye have no life in you* (John 6:53). He does not say that men have *a little life,* which by good management on their part may be brought to great strength and vigor. No, but he tells us that *he that believeth on the Son hath everlasting life: and he that believeth not the Son shall not see life; but the wrath of God abideth on him* (John 3:36). Without Christ, the description that God gives of the human soul is that it is *dead in trespasses and sins* (Ephesians 2:1); unless revived by the grace of God, it is forever bound in the chains of the second death.

Another reason water may be used as a figure for salvation is because of its cleansing properties. It is the cleansing element that we use in our homes and upon our persons. That man's soul is defiled by sin is not only a doctrine of revelation but also one of universal experience. God's holy eye looked down upon our world, and the verdict that he gave as to the state of our race was: *They are altogether become filthy* [corrupt]

(Psalm 53:3). For this universal corruption, a remedy has been provided in the blood of Jesus, which *cleanseth us from all sin* (1 John 1:7). But many, in the pride of their hearts, turn away from God's remedy and propose plans of their own invention. Some propose education and the general diffusion of knowledge as the remedy for the sins of the world.

Now, I would not say one word against education. Popular ignorance is more to be dreaded than the earthquake, the pestilence, or the famine. The ignorant man, though living amidst the refinements of civilization, is still half savage. But rest assured that no amount of education could ever purify the heart of man. The first of scholars has often been the first of villains; men whose splendid intellectual powers have excited the admiration of the world have been men of gigantic wickedness. The world is not as needy for talent as it is for moral purity. The chemist may be able to analyze the intoxicating cup and identify its deadly properties; the physician may be able to predict its bad effects upon the human system; and yet, both of them may be unrestrained drunkards. The soul of man needs not only to know what is right but also to love what is right. Nothing but the salvation through Christ can impart this. It alone can bring a double blessing – knowledge in the head and love in the heart. As God is both light and love, so the gospel, which comes from him, enlightens while it purifies.

But water may be used as a symbol of Christ's

> *The soul of man needs not only to know what is right but also to love what is right.*

salvation because of its *freeness*. How free to the whole race and how abundant the supply! As it rolls past us in the beautiful river, swells and sways in the magnificent lake, or leaps and dashes in the mountain torrent, how free it is to all! As the pure gift of God, it comes to us *without money and without price* (Isaiah 55:1). So it is with the salvation that is in the Savior. As that river of salvation rolls past us, the Lord's own proclamation is: *Whosoever will, let him take the water of life freely* (Revelation 22:17). Young and old, rich and poor, the learned and the ignorant, the bond and the free – all are pressed and plied by the urgency of inviting love to come. Oh sinner, if you only knew the gift of God and who is speaking to you, you would ask him for this living water this moment. Don't wait to bring a price in your hand to purchase what is offered to you as a gift, but come in the depth of your soul's poverty and be enriched with imperishable treasure.

What an impressive scene it was when God commanded Moses to strike the rock in the wilderness, and streams of refreshing water gushed out for the perishing people. About a million and a half human beings were perishing from their need for water, and as the hot wind passed over that scorched and burning plain where all vegetation was dying, it carried upon its wings the wild cry of human despair. By the direction of God, Moses took his stand beside the rock in Horeb and lifted the rod that was in his hand; he struck the rock three times, and behold, a clear, cool, refreshing stream of water gushed forth and rolled through the camp of Israel.

Imagine the joy that beamed from faces where only a few moments before, despair sat enthroned. Imagine mothers and fathers running with the precious water to their perishing children, the strong carrying it to their weak and dying neighbors and shouting the glad tidings in their ears! The Scriptures tell us that the striking of that rock and the result was a type of Christ: *And did all drink the same spiritual drink: for they drank of that spiritual Rock that followed them: and that Rock was Christ* (1 Corinthians 10:4).

Those beautiful waters that broke out from the rock in Horeb were *free for all the people.* They were not intended for one part of the people to the exclusion of the rest. Suppose, however, that a man came and took his stand beside the gushing waters with an empty pitcher in his hand. His eyes are bloodshot, his tongue cleaves to the roof of his mouth, and his whole appearance indicates extreme suffering from dehydration. But instead of dipping his pitcher in and drinking, he stands and says to himself, "I am a poor creature; I can do nothing by myself; I am perishing from my need for water, but I must wait for God's good time." He actually stands there expecting that in God's good time the water will flow up into his pitcher and fill it. How long do you suppose he would have to wait? Would God work another miracle to satisfy his whim and indulge his audacity in refusing to use the heaven-appointed means within his reach? No, we can see the folly of such conduct in worldly matters, and yet in spiritual things many may be following a similar course.

Jesus Christ, the Rock, was stricken for you. The

waters of salvation gush out for you. The Lord's own invitation to you is, *If any man thirst, let him come unto me, and drink* (John 7:37). And yet, instead of taking your Savior at his word and simply believing in him for your salvation now, you are waiting for some specially favored time to come and fit you for going to Christ by making your heart softer and purer than it is now! That time will never come, and your heart will become harder; you will drift further away from God the longer you stay away from Jesus. The only difference between one man and another in God's sight is that one has believed in the Lord Jesus and the other has not. Consider two men. One of them is a child of God, a joint heir with Christ, and a crown of glory in reserve for him with the favor of God shining upon his path. The other is under the curse of the law; the wrath of God remains on him, and if he dies in his present state, his soul will be lost as sure as the God of truth has spoken.

> *Unbelief alone fixes the great gulf between heaven and hell forever.*

What has made this vast difference? Simply, the one has believed in the Lord Jesus, and the other has rejected him. This alone will make the difference between those on the right hand and those on the left in the day of judgment. Unbelief alone fixes the great gulf between heaven and hell forever.

One day the people came to our Lord and said, *What shall we do, that we might work the works of God?* (John 6:28).

Jesus' reply was: *This is the work of God, that ye*

believe on him whom he hath sent (John 6:29). Not a single step can be taken heavenward until this is done.

I have seen an account of a conversation between a Christian gentleman and a young lady who was deeply anxious about her soul, that illustrates this point. She described herself as "uncertain about what to do."

"Why are you uncertain about what to do?" he asked.

She replied, "I have been coming every day to these meetings for four weeks, and all that time I have felt anxious about my soul; but all I do does not seem to make my situation any better."

"What do you try to do?"

"I have struggled to convince myself that I am a sinner – as I know I am. But though I know it, as a truth I do not feel about it as I should."

"How would you feel about it if you could?"

"I would have deep conviction."

"What is your present impression about yourself?"

"That I am a great sinner – that is all."

"And what more would you have?"

"That is what I do not understand. My next step should be for deeper conviction. But what more can I do?"

"Your mistake is a very common one," he replied. "Your next step, and only step, is to go to Christ, just as you are. Go to him at once. You can do nothing. Until now you have been relying upon yourself. Renounce all this as a dishonor done to Christ as a Savior, and go to him for all the help you need, hope for, or desire."

"Oh!" said she, as if a new light had dawned upon her mind. "Is that my next step?"

"Not your next, as if you had already taken one or more right steps in religion. Going to Christ is your first step and only step. He does not say, 'Come to conviction – come to a deeper sense of sin.' But he says, '*Come unto me*'" (Matthew 11:28).

She then exclaimed, "Oh! What a self-righteous creature I am! I see it all now. I have been refusing Christ, while all this time I thought I was preparing to come to him."

"Will you go to Jesus now?"

"I will," was the emphatic reply.

Suppose, after Moses struck the rock and the Israelites had seen the waters gush forth, they had not only refused to drink of these waters but had also gone and commenced striking another rock, determined to obtain water for themselves or perish. Their corpses would soon have lain around the rock, awful evidences of the danger of despising God's way of saving us and substituting our own. They might have been very sincere in their efforts to obtain water by their own works; they might have spent whole days and nights in the most earnest attempts to accomplish this, but their sincerity would not make the water flow or make the Almighty abandon his own plan and adopt theirs.

Paul bore witness to the sincerity of the Jews when they attempted to establish a righteousness of their own and would not submit themselves to the righteousness of Christ. He does not tell us that because of their sincerity God will accept their righteousness instead of Christ's. No, sincerity is not religion; it does not make error truth or change an act of human pride into an act well pleasing to God.

Over a river in Scotland, a strong stone bridge had been erected. Shortly after its completion, a furious storm of rain continued for several days and raised the waters of the river to a great height. The wild torrent came down with appalling force, bearing on its center the trunks of trees and huge blocks of wood. The arches of the bridge were filled with the rushing waters, and the strong structure seemed to shake under the pressure upon it. A crowd of persons was assembled on each side of the river, afraid to venture upon the bridge. They watched with intense anxiety when all at once a man on horseback galloped up, and before anyone could stop him, he rode to the very center of the bridge. There he stood and, in clear tones which rose above the roar of the tempest, exclaimed, "I am not afraid, my friends; I know it will not give way; I am sure it will stand." That man was the architect of the bridge, and he was boasting in the work of his own hands. To many people his confidence appeared foolishness, but the result proved that his trust was not misplaced.

What a rational ground of confidence the believer has in the work of the Lord Jesus!

What a far more rational ground of confidence the believer has in the work of the Lord Jesus! He feels that the foundation is perfect and can never give way. Amid the storms of coming wrath and the thunders of judgment, when great billows of fire shall be rolling across our globe, he shall be able to lift up his triumphant voice and say, *I know that my redeemer liveth* (Job 19:25). *I know* that he will *keep that which I have committed unto him against that day* (2 Timothy 1:12). Who shall lay anything to the charge of God's elect?

Chapter 10

The New Creature

The apostle Paul says, *If any man be in Christ, he is a new creature* (2 Corinthians 5:17). In previous chapters, I have shown that outside of Christ the sinner cannot really perform any good work, for *whatsoever is not of faith is sin* (Romans 14:23). Therefore, all attempts of men to make themselves holy before they come to Jesus will be a failure, and if persevered, will end in eternal disaster.

But it is equally true that if a sinner truly believes in the Lord Jesus, he will begin at once to abound in good works. The Lord Jesus has done a work *in* true Christians as well as a work *for* them, and he never saves from the guilt of sin without at the same time saving from its power. Accordingly, if believers are said to be elected, it is *through sanctification of the Spirit* (1 Peter 1:2). If they are said to be predestinated, it is *to be conformed to the image of his Son* (Romans 8:29). If they are said to be chosen, it is that they may *be holy and without blame before him in love* (Ephesians 1:4). In short, the only evidence a man can give that he has a living and not a dead faith is a holy life; for *faith worketh by love* and *purifieth himself* (Galatians 5:6; 1 John 3:3). An old writer remarks, "Say not that you have royal blood in your veins and are born of God unless you can prove your pedigree by daring to be holy."

If a man would rather –

- gossip at home or in his neighbor's house than go to a prayer meeting;

- run to hear fifty sermons than practice one;

- talk about ministers and criticize their performances than pray for their success or pay for their support;

- talk about a thousand sins of his brothers than subdue one in himself;

- read the newspaper or a novel than God's Holy Word; and

- finally, act as if Christ was very holy to save him the trouble of being holy himself,

he may rest assured that though he may pray with the earnestness of an Elijah, talk of feeling like a Daniel, and weep like a Jeremiah, all his religion is only the song of the hypocrite or the ravings of the self-deceiver.

Among the first evidences of the new creature in Christ Jesus is a love for the Bible. One of the most common remarks that ministers hear from the lips of young converts is, "Oh, sir, it seems like a new book!"

They may have been taught to read and reverence their Bible from their earliest years, and they may have committed large portions to memory in Sunday school and acquired a general knowledge of its contents. But, as soon as they believe in Jesus, they discover untold beauty that gleams from every page, and they exclaim with David, *O how love I thy law!* (Psalm 119:97).

This should not be surprising when we remember that the same Holy Spirit who inspired the Bible has now taken possession of their hearts, leading them not only to love it but also to open their eyes to discern *the things of the Spirit* (1 Corinthians 2:14). And I have no doubt that the reason why so much of the professed devotion of the present day is of such a stunted, dwarfish kind is that it is more public than private and is fed more by speeches about religion than by the pure, unadulterated Word of Truth itself.

If we read the memoirs of the martyrs and other holy men of God, whose undying examples reach us through the darkness of the centuries, we will find that their sturdy devotion, vigorous faith, and unbending principle gathered daily strength from reading and meditating on God's Word. If we read about the lives of the men most influential in the church of God in modern times, we will find that they were all emphatically Bible Christians. According to one individual, they drew the strength that enabled them from this holy source "to strike the kingdom of darkness with blows that resounded through eternity."

That devotion which is fed merely upon public meetings, narratives of personal experience, emotional hymns, sermons, and all that is exciting in religious gatherings will be found to be a poor, unsteady, sickly devotion indeed. While the devotion that draws its nourishment from the Bible will not only achieve the most good from public privileges, like the source from which it draws its life, it will also endure forever.

Permit an illustration not drawn from imagination. In a small cottage lives a poor widow, whose only son, a child for whom she prayed much, left her many years ago to enter upon the physical and moral dangers of a sailor's life. Since that time, she has heard nothing from her loved one and has long ago given him up for dead. One day her pastor is with her, directing her to the precious promises of the Bible, when a knock is heard at the door, and a letter is handed in. The widow perceives at a glance that it is the handwriting of her long-lost son. What a thrill she feels through her whole frame! What joy lights up her face as she exclaims, "My son is yet alive!" And with what eagerness she reads and lingers upon every word of that letter!

The devotion that draws its nourishment from the Bible will endure forever.

Suppose that when she discovered the handwriting of her son, she had laid the letter carelessly upon a shelf until the dust of weeks accumulated on it before she read it. Would she have shown any evidence of love for her son? Or suppose, after a long time, she took it down out of a sense of duty or desire to satisfy her conscience, yawning and dozing at the end pf each paragraph. Would this be any evidence of love for her son? No, whatever might be her occupation, you would know that there was not one spark of true motherly love in her heart if she were to do this.

The Bible is a letter from the Father of love, from whom we have been so long alienated. It speaks of the feelings of his heart toward us and tenderly invites us to return to the enjoyment of his favor. If we take no pleasure in reading it; if we are unwilling to make any sacrifices to understand it more fully; if we are delighted with the light and the trifling literature of the day and regard the Bible as dry and uninteresting, it is because *the love of the Father is not in [us]* (1 John 2:15).

My dear reader, cultivate an intimate and intelligent acquaintance with your heavenly Father's will. Study all of it, for it is all *profitable* (2 Timothy 3:16). As a good old Christian once remarked, "The Old Testament is the New Testament concealed, and the New Testament is the Old Testament revealed." It will be to us a guide through a world of darkness and perplexity, wiping the eye of sorrow, cheering the heart of sadness, and flashing the light of its glorious promises across the valley of the shadow of death.

Another evidence of the new creature is love for the Lord Jesus. An officer on the battlefield was engaged in personal conflict with an enemy when he slipped and fell to the ground. In an instant his opponent's sword was lifted for his destruction, but one of his men, who loved him, threw himself between him and the uplifted weapon, and it pierced him in his own heart. When the officer rose from the ground covered with the blood of the man who had laid down his life for him, wouldn't the emotion of love have filled his heart to overflowing?

It is not possible for anyone to believe that Jesus intervened between the sword of divine justice and his guilty heart, and then received in his own innocent heart the terrible blow that the sinner deserved, without feeling the kindness of a love that will be as permanent as God's throne. Therefore, all over the world and under all circumstances, Christians are able to say, *Lord, thou knowest all things; thou knowest that I love thee* (John 21:17).

It is said that after the Battle of Waterloo, a surgeon went to the field to aid the suffering and came to a French soldier who was badly wounded. As he began to probe the wound to find the fatal bullet, the dying man lurched with a convulsive effort and exclaimed, "A little deeper, and you will find the emperor," meaning his heart, and in his heart, a love for the emperor. So wherever you find a Christian, without respect to color or from the frigid to the scorching zone, you will find that the love of the Lord Jesus is deeper than the love of home, deeper than the love of kindred, and deeper than the love of life itself. One of the early Christians, when brought to the bar of Trajan, was asked, "Art thou a Christian?"

He replied, "I am; I have Christ in me." Trajan then asked him to deny Christ, but he exclaimed, "What? Shall I deny my Lord and Master? I have Christ in me." He was immediately led to martyrdom.

Among the first feelings produced by the belief of the gospel is joy, and the next is love. If a person were to rush into a burning building and save your life when you were in great danger, your first emotion would be joy because of your own deliverance. Your second emotion, as soon as you had time for reflection, would be that of gratitude to your deliverer. It is the reception of the gospel truth that makes the sinner happy and holy at the same time. *Faith which worketh by love and purifieth himself* (Galatians 5:6; 1 John 3:3).

Therefore, the young convert abandons the party scenes and worldly pleasures in which he played a conspicuous part, because he has ceased to have any enjoyment in them. His new-found joy in God and love for Jesus have given him new pleasures, as much superior to those of the world as the sun is to the glimmering light of a candle. His worldly friends think that the reason he has left their dancing parties and the exciting scenes of the theater is the dread of hell, the fear of censure from the church, or a desire to impress his new friends, but this is incorrect. He has ceased to find any pleasure where he formerly sought it so eagerly, and he has begun to drink of those rivers of pleasure that satisfy his soul forever.

> *It is the reception of the gospel truth that makes the sinner happy and holy at the same time.*

History tells us there was a deep trench around the walls of the ancient city of Babylon, which when opened, could absorb the waters of the great river Euphrates and leave its channel through the city dry. Likewise, the love of Christ has produced such a full and satisfying joy in the soul that all worldly channels of pleasure are left dry and worthless.

Whenever I hear professing Christians inquire about what harm there can be in dancing, in the theater, or in games of chance, I always know that it is a sign that the love of Christ is declining in their hearts, if indeed it ever existed at all. They are attempting to satisfy their conscience, which is virtually declaring that the bread of life with which Christ feeds the soul does not satisfy; therefore, they are anxious to find some excuse for getting back to the service of Satan.

Instead of arguing about the rightness or the wrongness of those things, which no truly spiritual mind has any doubt about, I would say, "Take heed, my brother, to your own heart. Your Lord has warned you not only against going back but also against even looking back; and you are instructed not to convey the impression of falling short. You are to shun the very appearance of evil, and the very fact that you are glancing with approval at the abounding iniquity of the world shows that your love for the Redeemer is waxing cold (Matthew 24:12). Take that cold heart back to Jesus, and don't rest until it is brimming over with his love, *who is holy, harmless, undefiled, [and] separate from sinners*" (Hebrews 7:26).

An anxious desire for the salvation of the perishing is evidence of the new creature in Christ Jesus.

An anxious desire for the salvation of the perishing is evidence of the new creature in Christ Jesus. Suppose that a stranger were to enter your house today. His clothes are plain and ordinary. His expression is kind and benevolent, but a solemn sadness fills his face, as if the shadow of some big sorrow were passing over it. This stranger begins to speak to you, and his words burn into your very heart. His conversation lifts your mind from the vain and the perishing and makes you feel as if you were hearing the echo of those enchanting choruses that fill the courts of heaven.

You are wondering who this stranger can be, when all at once your eyes are opened, and you see that you are in the presence of your Savior. He shows you the scars of those wounds he bore for you, and with that mild eye fixed upon you that broke Peter's heart, he asks you if you love him. With a trembling earnestness you answer, "Blessed Savior, I do love thee!" He tells you that all around you are dying sinners, and he has shed his precious blood for them and longs for their salvation with a depth of loving care which you cannot conceive. And then he asks you, as an evidence of your love for him, if you will go to them and tell them the story of his love and urge them to flee from the wrath to come. Christians, Jesus is thus speaking to you. The perishing are around you. They live in your houses, they eat at your tables; you mingle with them every day in the business of life. Oh, because you love the Lord Jesus and value an eternity of bliss, and because you wouldn't want to be found red from the blood of souls in the day of judgment, try to pluck them as *firebrand[s] plucked out of the burning* (Amos 4:11).

Chapter 11

Working for Jesus

It is a source of sublime satisfaction to reflect that the cause of Christ on earth is destined to enjoy a perfect triumph. We have the authority of God's Word for believing that as long as the sun shall shine and the moon sends her silvery beams across the world, the name of Jesus will thrill the human heart. The Lord whom we serve is building a spiritual temple upon the Rock of Ages, and *the gates of hell shall not prevail against it* (Matthew 16:18). Amid the rising and the falling of empires, amid the rush and the conflict of hostile parties, in spite of the unholy intrigues of political schemers and the proud boasts of infidel blasphemers, that temple will continue to increase in strength and loveliness until the topstone is brought forth amid shoutings of "Grace, grace."

But how is a result so glorious to be brought about? Not by a time-serving policy and a spirit of unholy compromise on the part of God's people; not by keeping quiet about the great truths of the gospel for which apostles contended, even unto death; not by splitting God's truth into portions and calling them essential and non-essential, important and unimportant, in order to suit the taste and gain the favor of a degenerate world. No, if truth is to triumph, it must be by the display of a spirit that is the very reverse of all this. This spirit bows with the most profound reverence before the whole revealed will of God and cherishes every part of gospel truth as its life and strength. It loves the whole body of the faithful, called by whatever name they may have, and while it sheds burning tears over a perishing world, it still adheres with stern resolution to the laws and established order of Christ's kingdom.

It is vastly important that we possess Christian love, which is preeminent of all the graces.

It would rather die a thousand deaths than yield up a single fragment of *the truth [as it] is in Jesus* (Ephesians 4:21). This is the Spirit of the great Captain of our salvation; this is the Spirit which inspired the faithful in all ages, and the man who possesses it leaves the impression of his own noble character upon society, and occupies the high and honorable position of a faithful witness for God.

Much is said about Christian love today and the necessity of its controlling our judgment on those who have a different opinion. It is vastly important that we possess that love, which is preeminent of all the graces and without which the most grandiose professions are only an empty name. But there is a principle which passes in society for Christian love that has nothing to do with love except for the name. True love is the child of heaven, but this one has its birth in the earth. True love rejoices in the truth; this one sacrifices truth to expediency. True love is hated by the world; this wicked one is rapturously applauded. True love discerns what is right and leaves consequences with God; this one thinks of consequences first and leaves the rightness to circumstances. True love *rejoiceth in the truth* (1 Corinthians 13:6). It boldly adheres to what is right rather than to what is popular; and undaunted by the cry of bias, which the ignorant and the cunning may raise, it *earnestly contend[s] for the faith which was once delivered unto the saints* (Jude 1:3). It says, "I fear God and I know no other fear."

I entreat you to cherish unshaken confidence in the power of truth. Truth in the hand of Jehovah is omnipotent; men may shackle it; they may imprison it; and they may bury it for a time amid the foulest errors and the most indecent and warped evils. But, loosen its shackles and give it room to work, and it will rise, fresh and immortal, and dispel everything around it that wants to give the impression of its own holy nature. The fact that error is so prevalent and seems to triumph takes nothing from the power of truth. Likewise, we could argue against the pervading nature of light, because there are many dungeons in the world that have never been visited by a single ray. We might darken our houses by shutting our doors and keeping the light from our windows out, but is this evidence that light is less powerful than darkness?

I fear many professing Christians today have very

little faith in the power of truth or in the overruling providence of God, for they will not breathe a syllable against popular error until they have measured and determined precisely the length and breadth of consequences. They want to know how far they may safely venture without giving offense. Why are men so afraid of consequences? If only they would but do their duty like Noah, Daniel, and Paul and trust God with the results! Why should we question God's faithfulness? Why should we act as if he were a Being who sees no distinction between right and wrong, and who is always ready to abandon the cause of truth and holiness which he has sworn to maintain? Why should we act as if he were in the habit of breaking his word to those who speak truth and work righteousness in their trying moments?

My prayer for you is that you may be bold for the truth and that a double portion of the Spirit of God may be given to you, so when the storms of the world begin to rage around you, you may feel the pleasant light of the Sun of Righteousness shining upon your soul and stand –

> As some tall cliff that lifts its awful form,
> Swells from the vale, and midway leaves the storm,
> Though round its breast the rolling clouds are spread,
> Eternal sunshine settles on its head.[7]

---

[7] Oliver Goldsmith, "The Deserted Village," 1770.

These lines present the picture of a "great head," rising superior to detraction, and fixing a single eye upon the Savior, while perplexed by the world's opposition. This is the picture as presented in the first Christian martyr – the devoted Stephen. Think of what that godly man saw when he forgave his enemies and *fell asleep. Behold,* said he, *I see the heavens opened, and the Son of man standing on the right hand of God* (Acts 7:56). He saw Jesus, not sitting but standing.

Now, it is written, *When he had by himself purged our sins, sat down on the right hand of the Majesty on high* (Hebrews 1:3); and when he ascended, as evidence that his work was accepted, the Father said to him, *Sit thou on my right hand, till I make thine enemies thy footstool* (Matthew 22:44).

But when Jesus looked down and saw the dauntless Stephen defending his cause single-handedly in the midst of bloody men, he stood up to receive and welcome the soul of his servant. Like Joseph with his brothers, he could no longer refrain himself. Oh, who can tell with what intense interest the Prince of martyrs stood and gazed upon the man who was proving faithful unto death! Glorious sight! Well might Stephen rejoice in spirit when he saw that almighty gush of tenderness toward him. He saw a Savior who more than died a thousand deaths for him, parted the sky, and made the way to heaven ready, for when he was ready to enter.

And what should hinder us from joining the chorus? Is the *Lamb slain* less worthy of our praises now than he will be hereafter? What should hinder us although we hear the hissing of the serpent everywhere around us? Let's drown his loud hissing with our louder praises. Those who work hardest for Jesus now and are least ashamed of him now will hereafter shine brightest in glory. While wickedness walks forth and reigns rampant, may Christians not be ashamed to acknowledge Christ's cause, not only in secret places but also in the face of day; not in whispers but loud enough to convince sinners that they are in danger. May Christians reveal that they fear the sinner's eternal destruction more than any reproaches they can cast on them.

At one time when Christians rose with the sun and sang the praises of the Lord, they made it the business of their lives to promote his glory. But *the god of this world,* not liking such practices, raised a storm and drove them into *dens and caves of the earth.* Satan cannot endure the thought that Christians should be as bold for Christ as sinners are for him, and rather than allow them to be so, he will move earth and hell to confuse and discourage them. He dreads to see believers stand up for God in the open. He knows the power of secret prayer, but he also knows that God will not answer prayer unless it is followed by action. When this is not the case, the prayer is insincere and cannot be heard. Let our prayers be accompanied by bold action, the bolder the better. Our Savior not only gives us the cup of life for ourselves but also promises us a reward if we help others to it. He offers a bonus in proportion to the activity of those who become

> *Satan dreads to see believers stand up for God in the open.*

coworkers with him in pleading with others to receive the cup of salvation.

If you do not wish to have the blood of souls upon you in the great day when the Master appears, then be faithful now in presenting the Savior to all you are able to influence. To be privileged to tell the glad story of the cross, and stand between the eternal God and perishing men as they rush to their punishment, and entreat them to be reconciled to God is the most solemn work that man can engage in on this side of the eternal world. This work is not committed to ministers alone, for the Lord says, *Let him that heareth say, Come* (Revelation 22:17). The people with whom you come in contact daily are not the creatures of a day, whose dirge is to be sung when the light of life forsakes their eyes. A lighthearted hymn is not to be played over them when they reach the boundary line that separates time from eternity, for that may cause you to have some excuse for your indifference. But they are to live as long as God lives, in bliss unspeakable or in misery which no one can imagine.

They are now living in the midst of the light of the gospel, which permits no neutrality and must prove the delight of life or of death to their souls. It may depend upon you whether they are to be saved or lost. This great responsibility Jesus puts upon you! An angel might tremble under this responsibility, and our minds would fall with a crushing weight if the same Lord who gives the command does not also promise strength for its performance.

Besides, he only asks us to go and tell his truth; he

does not ask us to go and be successful, for success is his work, not ours. The sinner may scorn your message and fling back the truth you utter with a proud contempt, but the fact that you have warned him with tearful earnestness and with a loving heart will acquit you of all blame in the day of the Lord.

One beautiful summer afternoon, a father went out to walk in the fields with his little daughter, a child of four or five years of age. While the little one amused herself in picking flowers and chasing butterflies, the father sat down under the shadow of a tree and fell asleep. He only slept a short time, but when he awoke, his loved one was nowhere to be seen. He urgently called her name, but only an echo answered his voice. Discovering a precipice at one side of the field, he rushed to its edge and gazed over; to his horror, he saw the corpse of his dear child, her fair hair stained in her own blood.

Who can imagine the anguish of that father? He blamed himself for her death and in wild and frantic words called himself her murderer. It was a heavy burden upon his mind until his dying day. Dear parent, take heed that you do not slumber and sleep in spiritual indifference while your dear children are dropping into hell! If their bodies are suffering, you eagerly run for medical aid and hang over them in deep anguish. Oh, do not neglect the disease of the soul! Send for the Great Physician in believing and persistent prayer, saying, *Come down ere my child die* (John 4:49). He will hear you and make your children God's children and heirs of eternal glory.

Chapter 12

The Gospel Feast

I have now set before you the world's hope as seen in Christ crucified. The great feast of God's love has been spread before you, and I have urged you to partake. *O taste and see that the LORD is good* (Psalm 34:8). What you do with this invitation is a matter of deep, heartfelt anxiety. Will you reject it or receive it? Your eternal well-being hangs upon your decision. I am reminded of our Lord's parable of the great marriage feast and the man who came without a proper garment. Note the lessons taught by that instructive parable in Matthew 22:11-12: *And when the king came in to see the guests, he saw there a man which had not on a wedding garment: and he saith unto him, Friend, how camest thou in hither not having a wedding garment? And he was speechless.*

Our blessed Savior uses one of his striking parables here to show God's dealings with his creatures, both under the old and the new dispensations. A great king is represented as preparing a feast for the marriage of his son. The king sent a general call to certain invited guests to come to the banquet because everything was ready. They, however, treated the call with contempt and went their ways, one to his farm and another to his merchandise. Others laid hold of the king's servants, treated them shamefully, and even put some of them to death. Against such vile and ungrateful conduct, the king's resentment flamed forth, and he sent out his armies to destroy the murderers and to burn up their cities.

But because those first invited proved themselves unworthy and ungrateful, is the feast to be unattended and lost? No, he again commissions his servants to go out with a free, general invitation to all to come to the feast. They went to the highways and used the most pressing invitations to fill the banquet room. This is done; the guest chamber is filled; and the king comes in to see his company. He notices one solitary individual who is not arrayed in a wedding garment. He demands to know the reason for this strange neglect, but the offender is speechless. He does not have a word of excuse, so the king orders him to be bound hand and foot and cast into outer darkness.

Our Lord's lesson in this parable is not difficult to see. The Jews had been a chosen, peculiar people, to whom God had committed his holy laws and to whom a long line of prophets and holy men had been sent to invite them to come to God's banquet of love. Many messengers who came with Jehovah's message on their lips were treated with the fiercest scorn and even put to death. The gracious Savior and his apostles invited them to the feast with no better result. Still God treated them with amazing patience and longsuffering; after the crucifixion of our Lord, when the full atonement had been made by the slaying of the Lamb and in a special sense the feast might be said to be ready, he renewed the invitation in a most compelling form. The apostles were commanded to begin at Jerusalem, the capital of their nation, and offer them salvation. Yes, the very men who had nailed the holy Redeemer to the cross and whose hands were red with the blood of murder had the offer of free forgiveness through the blood of the cross. God had sent his own Son to them, and they had rejected him and treated him with the most malignant hate. But that rejected, despised Savior still invites them through the lips of his servants to come to him, and the streets of Jerusalem echo the glad tidings.

But all this wealth of love is displayed in vain. The last messengers are treated even worse than the first. They became enraged at the very offer of pardon, because it implied guilt, which they were too proud to acknowledge. At last the extent of their iniquity was realized, and the wrath of the great king blazed forth against them. He sent avenging armies against them, and their beautiful city was burned. Fearful retaliation came upon them. Abandoned to their own vile passions, conflict, petty jealousy, and ungovernable rage, wild anarchy took possession of the people. Thousands upon thousands perished miserably by famine and battle, while the rest were dispersed as wanderers and vagabonds among all lands, covering every shore with the fragments of a nation's shipwreck.

But the great king would not allow his prepared feast to be unattended. His servants went to the highways and hedges with an unlimited invitation. No longer confined to the Jews, or to the people of any one nation, the invitation was to the whole world: *Come; for all things are now ready* (Luke 14:17). To the Jews the awful words had been uttered: *Seeing ye . . . judge yourselves unworthy of everlasting life, lo, we turn to the Gentiles* (Acts 13:46). The whole world was to be the field of work for God's messengers, and salvation was to be published in all the highways of the earth to all men.

Some may come into the guest chamber, Christ's visible church, who are not Christians and don't have the robe of the Savior's righteousness on them. But the glance of Christ's eye is on them, and though they may deceive their fellow man, they cannot deceive him. This man was among those who seem to think that being in Christ's church is as good as being in Christ himself.

Sadly, many are in the world of suffering who were only in the outward church when living on the earth. They heard the Word of God with deep attention; they abandoned many outward sins; they enjoyed a warm interest in religious matters. Parents and ministers were encouraged and spoke of them as Christians; they were encouraged to unite with the church. They may even have been elevated to official positions in the house of God until at last God in his providence tested them, placing them in circumstances that developed their true character and proved that the root was not in them.

An egg and an eggshell are very different, but at a little distance they look very much alike. Likewise, a man who only has an empty profession of faith may appear as well as the man who has Christ in his heart, the hope of glory. But when the testing time comes, which God is sure to send, the difference will be made most apparent.

Standing on the mountaintop in the summertime and looking at the forest clothed in its beautiful mantle of green, you could not distinguish the evergreens from the other trees; but after the cold, bleak, wolfish winds of winter come, you will see the difference. So it is in a church when all is prosperous. A popular minister fills the pulpit, and crowds constantly fill the place of worship. Great numbers are from time to time added to their ranks, and the financial affairs of the church are easy. It acquires the reputation of being the leading religious interest in the area. Then it is very difficult to tell the empty professors of faith from the true believers.

> *A man who has an empty faith may appear as well as the man who has Christ in his heart. But when the testing time comes, the difference will be made apparent.*

But let a *sifting time* come – let the popular preacher leave; let divisions and bitter animosities enter their counsels; let financial difficulties press upon that tender and sensitive part of man, his finances, and soon it will be apparent who the superficial professors are. The true Christians then emerge in all their glory; they stand by the church with a warmer affection and a more steadfast zeal the more their trials and troubles increase. *Like a tree planted by the rivers of water, that bringeth forth his fruit in his season; his leaf also shall not wither* (Psalm 1:3). The testing time reveals which are the evergreens.

Two houses stand on the bank of a beautiful stream. From the outside they seem equally good. They have stood there for years, answering all the purposes of a comfortable home to their respective owners. But a testing time comes at last. The stream swells one dark night, far beyond its usual proportions. It overflows its banks, and with a wild uproar, its dark, angry waves beat upon those two houses. In the midst of the howling of the winds and the furious dashing of the waters, a despairing cry of human voices comes from one of the houses. It has begun to shake and break up under the pressure of the surging billows, and soon it moves into the angry waters, with its vulnerable inhabitants who trusted in it, to join the accumulating pile of rubbish that marks their destructive course. This house was built upon the sand, so it could not stand the time of trial; the other stood firm, for it was founded upon a rock.

The testing time will eventually come to every man. It is right that it should. Under its sifting power there may be the blasting of many hopes, hopes made strong by the culture and indulgence of many years. Some who seemed to be pillars in the house of God may prove to have been rotten pillars, only covered with a little paint and varnish; but God's true people will stand unmoved under every trial. The severest test will have no more effect upon them than the fluttering of the insect's wing upon the hard granite rock. *The foundation of God standeth sure* (2 Timothy 2:19).

We recently saw a boy proudly exhibit what he thought was a silver dollar. It was bright and beautiful, and he spoke with delight of what it would buy. But when the "testing time" came, and he presented it at the counter of the store, it was found to be counterfeit. He wept bitterly, but all the tears in the world could not change the worthless thing into silver. In the same way, the only hope that will pass at heaven's bank is a hope founded solely in the death and righteousness of Jesus.

When I think of the worth of your soul, the tremendous peril to which you are exposed, the powerful means you have resisted, and the hardening process in your mind, I see you standing on a precipice, drawn downward by the horrid fascination of sin. I long to compel you to come in, but how are you to be compelled? Friends cannot do it; ministers cannot do it; churches cannot do it. Vast armies and the power of kings cannot do it; it is not a physical compulsion, but the tender, holy compulsion of love – the love of Christ, that can do it. This has been offered to you and is being offered now. If it fails, all fails. If this does not draw you in, you will be left out forever.

The test that was applied to the man at the wedding concerned one single point, namely, possessing a wedding garment. We understand this to be the garment of Christ's righteousness. If we are covered with that, all will be well; if not, we shall be covered with confusion. The king did not investigate his past life, whether he had been a great sinner or not, whether he had a good moral reputation, or whether he had violated all the decencies of society; the one fault for which he was cast out was not having on a wedding garment. This was the testing point.

To understand this better, we should remember that it was a Jewish custom of a marriage festival to offer each guest a suitable garment as he entered. They did not provide garments for themselves, for men called in from the highways might plead that they had no proper garment as an excuse. Therefore, this man was speechless. He had no excuse to offer. The king knew, and he knew himself, and all in the assembly knew that it was entirely his own fault that he appeared as he was – that a garment had been offered, but he rejected it.

So it is in the gospel feast. We are not required to dress ourselves, to fit ourselves for appearing before God; we are only required to put on the holy garb of righteousness that has already been provided for us. So, in the end, if we are found by the great King to be clothed in our own filthy rags, we will not have a word of excuse to offer but will be covered with shame and everlasting turmoil. How effectually does this answer the objection of those who, when urged to come to Christ, say, "I am not good enough yet!" Very true; and you never will be good enough.

For that very reason, God has provided a way by which you can come, independent of your goodness. "But," says one person, "I am not at all satisfied with myself." I hope you never will be.

The Bible does not say, "Being satisfied with ourselves, we have peace with God," but it does say, *Being justified by faith, we have peace with God, through our Lord Jesus Christ* (Romans 5:1). Satisfaction with ourselves, our faith, our motives, or our works are not being proposed for us, but satisfaction with Christ is. This verse does not speak of peace that arises from an exalted opinion of oneself but from an exalted concept of the fullness that is in Christ.

If on the day of judgment you do not have the robe of Christ's righteousness, you will not be able to plead that you had no opportunities of obtaining it. You will know, and an assembled world will know, and all men and angels will know that it has been offered to you repeatedly, and you would not accept it. The Spirit labored, the Bible urged, ministers preached, friends entreated, conscience rebuked, and all in vain! Oh, poor soul, will you to sink into the whirlpool of God's wrath in the end, while the lifeboat of salvation is near enough to save you? When the earth reels back and forth, when the heavens are on fire, and the stars are falling in the light of a burning world, you will curse your folly and madness in neglecting to clothe yourself in the spotless robe that Christ has provided.

If on the day of judgment you do not have the robe of Christ's righteousness, you will not be able to plead that you had no opportunities.

Why not come now, even while your eyes are upon this page, and cast your sins on Jesus? He atoned for:

- sins of every name and of every color,
- sins against light and knowledge,

- sins against the law and the gospel,
- sins of omission and commission, and
- sins of youth, middle age, and old age.

All have been laid upon Jesus.

The blessed Savior has suffered for your sins that are too numerous to number and no eloquent speech could describe, dark and black in their moral depravity. Freely and fully you will be pardoned. Your guilt will be taken away; your calling and election will be sure; your serene and joyful soul will delight to follow the Lamb wherever he leads; and with the blood-washed multitude that has been gathered from the world's highways, you will sit down at the marriage supper of the Lamb.

An emphatic part of this parable is that this man was cast out because he lacked one thing. There was no long catalog of sins and imperfections for which he was to be condemned. If he had possessed that one thing, all would have been well. So it is with faith in the Lord Jesus Christ. *He that believeth not is condemned already* (John 3:18). A watch without a mainspring, a ship without a helm or a compass, a row of ciphers without a code, such is the soul that has no faith in Christ. There may be many good things about a man, but the one thing lacking is the vital thing. Unbelief is the cause of every sin, the grand root of all iniquity in the human soul. It is the damning sin that is filling hell with victims and robbing souls of happiness here and eternal joys hereafter. It is the God-dishonoring sin of unbelief. Faith secures the garment of Christ's righteousness to the soul and ensures its admittance into the heaven of purity and love where God and holy spirits dwell. There, in the language of the poet –

> Out of your last home, dark and cold,
> Thou shalt pass to a city whose streets are gold;
> From the silence that falls upon sin and pain,
> To the deathless joys of the angels' strain,
> Well shall be ended what ill begun,
> Out of the shadow into the sun.

I would call attention to the conduct of the man without the wedding garment. He made no excuses; he uttered no protests; he was speechless. This is very solemn and impressive, far more awful than if we had been told that he uttered a wild shriek of despair. His recklessness and madness causing his tongue to cleave to the roof of his mouth strikes us as something much more revealing than words. The wicked rushing about in uncontrollable anguish and calling upon the rocks and the hills to fall upon them does not impress us as strongly as this man's speechless anguish. At present, sinners have enough excuses to make and find plenty of words to defend themselves to their fellow man for not becoming Christians. When we urge them to accept a Savior's gracious offers without delay, they tell us of the hypocrisy of professed Christians, the pressure of their worldly cares, the temptations to which they are exposed, the strength and intensity of their natural passions, the vagueness of the Word of God, and a long list of other excuses. But when they shall come to stand before God and feel his eye looking at them through and through, it will be quite different. They will be struck dumb in his presence.

They will then know that God will not listen to excuses but to reasons. And even now the sinner knows that he has no reasons to give. But in the light of eternity, this will be more fully felt. His memory will bring up all his past privileges:

- every solemn warning he has received,
- every sermon to which he has listened,
- every Sabbath when God has come near him in love,
- every time the Spirit has pursued him,
- every alarming foresight that has startled him from his indifference, and
- every vow and promise and resolution that has been broken.

These, with all the events of his life, will be present with him and paralyze his tongue into silence. Memory will be inconceivably strengthened in eternity. All of our words, thoughts, actions, and privileges will be recalled. Our whole past history will be vividly before us.

Today, the sinner forgets his sins as fast as he commits them; but then, he will remember them, distinct and awful, in all their aggravations of being committed against light and knowledge. Children of devout parents will remember their counsels, their tears, and their prayers as they labored for their salvation. The times of family prayer, the spiritual books given to them, and the religious meetings to which they were taken will all be recalled with the vividness of a present reality. Oh, if they have all been in vain, how the memory will sting through all eternity! Imagine eternity spent counting Sabbaths lost, privileges abused, and parental instructions trampled upon. Imagine hearing again from memory the truths mocked when they were first heard! And then, the realization that it is now forever too late to derive any benefit from these truths silences the tongue. "Hell is truth seen too late."[8]

> *Imagine eternity spent counting Sabbaths lost, privileges abused, and parental instructions trampled upon.*

There is one day in which you can be saved, and that is the day of salvation. There is one way in which you can be saved, and that is through faith in Jesus. When the huge billows of the flood surged around the globe, there was one ark of safety. There was one means of deliverance for the people of Israel when the destroying angel passed on his mission of death at the dark midnight hour. When the fiery serpents scattered death through the camp of the Israelites, there was one brazen serpent lifted up with healing power. Only one rock sent forth refreshing waters. On the great Day of Atonement, one scapegoat carried the people's sins away. In like manner, there is one name given under heaven among men by which we can be saved – even the name of Jesus (Acts 4:12). And there is one thing a sinner can do to be saved – believe in that precious Savior.

---

8   Thomas Hobbes, *Leviathan*, 1651.

Remember that anxious father who came to the Lord Jesus with a burden of grief. About twelve years before, God had given him a very precious gift, a little daughter, and every day since, he had learned to prize the gift more and more. The house that had so often been made happy by her innocent chatter and merry laughter was now silent and sad, for the little girl was dying. The distressed father had heard of the wonder-working Savior, and in his deep anguish he said, "I will go to him."

And Jesus said to him, *Be not afraid; only believe* (Mark 5:36). It was as if he had said, "Only trust me, and I will attend to all the rest." So it is with you. Jesus has left you nothing to do but simply to trust in his finished work. Only believe, and all will be well with your soul forever. Ponder solemnly your position before God. Are you found with the garment of Christ's righteousness upon you, or do you lack that one needful thing? God's best, greatest, most precious gift is offered to you; do you prefer your own filthy rags? In yourself, you can never find any merit on which God can receive you into his eternal home. You can never live such that the eternal Holy One will pronounce you blameless.

So, come and accept that spotless robe of Jesus, in which you will be presented faultless before God. Only believe and trust your eternal safety to Christ. We are told that in a public school in New York, the fire alarm rang out. A terrible panic ensued; a rush was made for the doors, and one of the teachers, a young lady, was injured by jumping from a window. In the midst of the furious panic, one little girl did not move; when order had been restored, she was asked how she could sit so still and be so calm when all the others were in terror. "My father," said she, "is a fireman; and he told me if there was a fire alarm in the school, I must just sit still." This was true faith in a father's word and wisdom. She believed, and it gave her sweet peace.

> Still there is room in the banqueting hall –
> Room at the Gospel feast, still room for all;
> To the table though millions already have come,
> Still there is room for more – still there is room.
> Then go call the lame, and the halt, and the blind,
> For all things are ready. The table is spread
> With the wine, and the oil, and the heavenly
>   bread.
> The bread and the oil are the choicest, the best;
> And the wine from the fruit of the True Vine is
>   pressed.
> Such dainties no storehouse on earth can afford;
> The storehouse of heaven has furnished the board,
> Nor will it be drawn while a guest you can find
> 'Mong the outcast, the hungry, the lame and the
>   blind.
> To the streets, then, and lanes of the city repair,
> To the dismal retreats of crime, vice, and despair;
> Go to the highways and byways of sin,
> And the wretched and houseless compel to come in.

Even with all the bluster of infidelity in the present day, I do not think that our chief danger arises from that source. Worship of some kind is natural to man; he will have a religion of some kind, but the great tendency today is for a religion of mere ceremony.

We have little understanding of the struggle that an intelligent Jew like Paul, for example, had to go through when he gave up the splendid forms and ritualistic pomp of Judaism for the severe simplicity of gospel truth. He was accustomed to crowds of priests, smoking sacrifices, ornaments of the temple all ablaze with gold, and the artifacts and divine origin of all that met the eye. The fire still burned in the temple that had not been extinguished for fifteen hundred years, which impressed the imagination and fired the patriotism of a devout descendant of Abraham.

If a person knows something of the power of these things, let him visit some of those splendid cathedrals of Europe where everything appeals to the senses. The lofty arched roof, the massive pillars, the highly ornamented windows, the white-robed officials, the chants, and the mighty swell of the organ that seems to shake the old, gray wall exert an overpowering influence upon the feelings and the imagination.

The glory of the gospel does not appeal to the senses in this way; it is the whisper of divine love in the soul. It comes with a mighty power, for it is the power of God. It doesn't glare in the eye or the ear of the multitude, but *cometh not with observation* (Luke 17:20). It does what nothing else can – it saves the soul. The holy, spiritual, awakening thought that comes to the sinner – he scarcely knows how – produces a greater revolution than those that agitate nations and overthrow dynasties, because it saves his eternal soul.

It is the gospel of love; it fills the heart where enmity was natural, and love is never pompous. When the mother watches by the crib of her dying baby, night after night, she does not proclaim her great sacrifices to the world, but loves to be alone with her God and her heavy sorrow. During our Lord's earthly days, ritualism abounded, and teachers of religion could not fast, nor pray, nor give alms without letting all Jerusalem know what wonderfully good people they were. Our Lord had the tenderest words and most loving promises for the vilest transgressors that came to him in repentance, but for these hypocrites he had terrible warnings and righteous denunciations that fell among them like thunderbolts.

Our Lord had the tenderest words and most loving promises for the vilest transgressors that came to him in repentance.

The gospel teaches us to go forth doing good every day, because the loving heart supplies the forceful motive. It leads us to do good because we are God's children, not because we wish to be thought so. The very nature of the good tree is to bear fruit, but the chief source of strength and fruitfulness is out of sight.

The gospel is expansive and progressive in the human soul. The religion of rites, and forms, and ceremonies does not grow with our growth. It does not become brighter to the perfect day. It goes on, age after age, depending upon the same performances. No matter what the circumstances, it drones on with its vain repetitions. The gospel has milk for babies and strong meat for men. It offers sweet, gentle truths to woo the young; massive, strong doctrines for the most gifted intellects; and promises great and precious for the aged.

The religion of ritualism is a strong device of Satan to satisfy the human soul with a sham. It says God does not look at the heart but is zealous about the outward appearance. It seeks to satisfy the soul that begins to feel its dreadful loss in departing from God with the jingle and the rattle of a few childish toys. It seeks to represent God himself as well pleased with empty parades and gaudy trappings. It is the religion of human nature in its deepest depravity, and it sends souls into eternity in teeming crowds with lies that envelope them like a garment.

The soul enlightened from on high and convicted of sin by the Holy Spirit will not be held long by a religion of formality. You may please a hungry child with toys for a while, but as the hunger grows, and the child becomes noisier and insistent, nothing but substantial bread will do. So none but Jesus can satisfy helpless sinners. He is the Bread of Life, and nothing but a personal acceptance of him by faith can satisfy the hunger of the soul. It is a real feast, not a mere picture of one, to which he invites us. To hunger and thirst after righteousness is the sure precursor of that blessed state, where we are filled with the fullness of God and where we shall awake in his likeness.

Many of the blessings of Christianity lie in the future, for *it doth not yet appear what we shall be* (1 John 3:2), but real and imperishable blessings are now in the Christian's possession. He is now God's child, and prayer is speaking to his Father; repentance is returning to his Father; and faith is resting on the love of his Father. When he looks up to those heavens that seem to shelter our earth and sees the myriads of stars that gleam in the darkness of night, his soul is thrilled with the thought of the vastness of his Father's possessions.

One who rejoices in God in this relationship longs to bring all wanderers back to their Father. The heart touched by God's love loves others, just as the iron that has felt the power of the magnet becomes magnetic itself.

We see this in the apostle John. Love was the very soul of his religion, the element in which he lived, the glory of his teaching, and the charm of his society. We have heard of the sculptor who, seeing a rough, unhewn block of marble, exclaimed, "What a glorious statue you conceal!" So the Christian looks upon the lowest, most degraded of human beings, and sees one capable of being made a child of God, an heir of heaven, a companion of angels. He knows that the roughest block of humanity can be made into the likeness of Christ by the Holy Spirit, and he prays and labors for this.

The apostle, while rejoicing in his present privileges, looked forward to something greater. A rich man may adopt a poor beggar from the streets into his family. He may have him washed, dressed, educated, and permit him to call him father. He may leave him all his property, but there is one thing he cannot do – he cannot give him his nature; he cannot impart his own likeness to him. But when God adopts us into his family through Jesus, he makes us partakers of his own nature and impresses us with his image. Men notice that we have been with Jesus. The spirit and the temper of the Holy One shines out of us, somewhat imperfectly but still in a way that shows the divine relationship that has been formed.

What will add so much to the bliss of heaven is that this likeness will be perfect. No sinful passion shall ever again fill the soul with sorrows and remorse. We will do good without sin being present with us, and the song of grateful love shall gush forth uninterrupted. Oh, blessed hope! The hope of being like Jesus! How it should dignify our lives now. We must seek to be of one mind with God, hating what he hates, loving what he loves, judging things by his standard. We should strive to be meek, loving, gentle, and unselfish, as the blessed Savior was. We should stand up as bold and unflinching witnesses, as he was; we should stoop to any work, however lowly, so that he may serve others through us. Think of being like Jesus and with Jesus forever.

We must seek to be of one mind with God, hating what he hates, loving what he loves.

We have known many happy moments with Jesus and his people on earth, but they do not last. Sin comes like a great darkness and separates us from God. But eternity will be the crown of our glory. If we could look forward millions of ages and see an end to our enjoyment, it would cast a dampness upon our bliss, a dark shadow over our brightness. But we will be forever with the Lord, and forever like the Lord. Oh, what wondrous love this is! We can live as long as God lives and with his mighty love overflowing in our hearts – all for nothing, all of grace, free grace.

Surely if we can resist all that God has freely offered and give up our powers for the love of the world, we can expect nothing but to hear, when we enter eternity, that terrible blast of condemnation: *Depart from me, ye cursed* (Matthew 25:41).

A man who had been born blind had his eyes operated on by a skillful ophthalmologist so that he could gradually see objects around him. For the first time he looked into the faces of his wife and children; his own face beamed with love. At last he exclaimed, "Oh, why have I seen these faces before I've seen him whose skill opened my eyes? Show me the doctor." Thus the redeemed shall wish first to see Jesus.

* * * *

One of the most solemn, most searching, and most humbling questions is from the lips of our Lord – *Lovest thou me?* It is a deep disgrace to us, a burning shame, that after all he has done for us, he should still have to ask such a question. No wonder our wretched ingratitude causes the awful words to roll over our heads like a peal of thunder: *If any man love not the Lord Jesus Christ, let him be Anathema Maranatha* [accursed] (1 Corinthians 16:22).

Christ's love, as revealed on the cross and believed with the whole heart, is the only power that can sweep the world of its impurities. Wherever it is faithfully preached, it changes the whole nature of society. Savages hear of it, and it lifts them to the dignity of God's children. Idolaters hear of it, and their idol temples are deserted. His love humbles the proud and elevates the humble. It teaches citizens their rights and obligations, and rulers their solemn responsibilities. It emboldens the timid and renders invincible the brave. It smooths the wrinkles on the brow, binds up the broken heart, and dispels despair as it sits brooding over the desolations of the grave. Christ's love transforms the slave of passion and sin into Christ's freeman.

The doctrine of Christ crucified penetrates into the immoral hangouts in our cities, where misery in its most hideous forms astounds the heart of the beholder, and instantly there is a great change. It goes into the cell of the criminal whose soul is stained with crimes, which no heart could even imagine, and it melts his hard heart into tender repentance.

Wherever Christ's love is faithfully preached, it changes the whole nature of society.

Amidst the roar of battle, it comes to the dying soldier and gives him a peace that is unspeakable and full of glory. It comes to the sailor in the middle of the midnight tempest, when his proud ship is thrown as a wreck on the boundless deep, or when the rocks are strewn with the fragments of her perishing strength, and enables him to cast the anchor of his hope. In short, it comes to every human heart that will receive it and imparts a confidence that can never be shaken, world without end.

When a dying lady heard some of her friends say in a whisper, "She is sinking fast," she opened her eyes and said, "How can I sink through a rock?" She felt that she was resting on the Rock of Ages. All who are not on that Rock are on the shifting sand, which the storms of judgment will sweep from under them.

Many voices unite to urge you to come to Christ. The eternal Father says, *This is my beloved Son: hear him* (Luke 9:35). The Holy Spirit urges you to come to Christ to avoid the peril of your precious soul. Conscience lifts up its awful voice and calls you to flee from the wrath to come. The voices of loving people, who have often prayed for you on earth in tender memories from the eternity into which they have gone, urge you to come to the Savior they love. A great cloud of witnesses encompasses you and by the most tremendous motives urges you to a happy decision. I now entreat you to come at once to our adorable Redeemer – the world's hope.

Robert Boyd
– A Brief Biography

Robert Boyd was born on August 24, 1816, in Girvan, South Ayrshire, Scotland. Robert grew up learning the ways of God. He learned to pray every morning and evening. He memorized the entire book of Psalms and other entire chapters of the Bible. He also spent much time reading good Christian books, *The Pilgrim's Progress* being one of them.

When Robert was about twelve years old, his family moved to Glasgow. Robert's spiritual life began to suffer, as he made some friends who led his heart away from God. God was looking out for Robert, though, and brought him back to Himself. When Robert was about fifteen years old, he went to hear a preacher who was plain and direct and full of Christ, and it was then that Robert gave his heart and life to Jesus. He left his ungodly friends and got more involved in Christian activities.

Robert became sick for a while, but used the time to read many Christian books by men such as Ralph Erskine, Thomas Boston, John Flavel, Richard Baxter, and John Bunyan. Robert Boyd began to prepare himself for what he believed God had for his life's work – to be a minister of the gospel. However, when Robert's father suddenly died, Robert had to give up his studies and find work. He was employed to go around and speak on behalf of the growing temperance movement, encouraging people to abstain from alcohol.

He also began doing missionary work in the city. He began giving talks during the week and preaching on Sundays, where his preaching resulted in spiritual awakening. Robert joined a Baptist church in Stirling, where he soon became the new pastor after the former pastor suddenly died. Robert wanted to proclaim Christ Jesus in every sermon. "I did not like to preach a single sermon without explaining how a sinner can be saved," he said. Robert Boyd was determined to live his life fully for God and to always be in close communion with Him.

On April 6, 1840, Robert Boyd married Christina Forbes. Robert and Christina had nine daughters, one of whom died in infancy in Scotland. Boyd continued his pastoral and temperance work in Stirling, as well as undertaking evangelistic work in and around Edinburgh. His health began to suffer, and he tried to find strength and rest by visiting the seashore, but his health did not improve. He made the difficult decision to go to North America.

Upon arriving in Montreal, Canada, on September

25, 1843, Boyd began preaching. He became the pastor of a new Baptist church in Brockville, Ontario. After pastoring there for seven years, Boyd spent five years pastoring a church in London, Ontario, before accepting a call to a Baptist church in Hamilton, Ontario. However, his poor health still troubled him. His father-in-law had recently died and had left them his small farm, so the Boyds soon moved to the farm in Waterville, Wisconsin, where he rested for about ten months, obeying the doctor's orders.

Boyd then traveled ten miles back and forth every weekend to preach at a Baptist church in Waukesha, Wisconsin, but soon moved his family to Waukesha where he could more fully carry out his pastoral duties. In 1856, Boyd visited some friends in Chicago, taking time to preach there too. Some who heard him preach had been considering starting a church in the southern part of the city, and they thought Boyd was the right man for the job. So in September 1856, the Boyds moved to Chicago.

Boyd's communion with God and desire for the lost led to many conversions and times of revival wherever he preached. As he began pastoring in Chicago, there was so much interest in spiritual things that Boyd held meetings every night for months, and people met to pray every morning. There were also meetings at noon, and Boyd spent the afternoons visiting people to discuss their souls. He speaks of this time as the happiest time of his life.

However, his health again suffered. He spent a few months near Cleveland seeking rest and healing. Upon his return to Chicago, he resumed his labors, and in 1862, the congregation moved to a larger building on the corner of Wabash Avenue and 18th Street. Boyd continued what pastoral duties he could, and he also ministered to Confederate prisoners.

Boyd often had to preach while sitting down, and even had to be carried in to preach at times. He soon resigned from his pastoral position. During his twenty-seven years as a pastor, he had preached more than eleven thousand sermons, in addition to giving other talks and lectures. He had also officiated at about six hundred funerals, five hundred weddings, and had personally baptized 869 converts.

Robert Boyd then moved back to Waukesha, where his health soon improved so much that he agreed to preach once a week at the Baptist church there. Due to some paralysis in his legs, he still had to be carried in and out and still preached from a chair, but he was glad to have the opportunity to preach once again. Boyd preached in the morning one day in September 1867, and then traveled to Pewaukee to preach in the afternoon, where he would preach his last sermon. He caught a severe cold on the way home, and the inflammation of his spine that he had struggled with for many years led to the partial paralysis that confined him to bed for the rest of his life.

Due to his inability to continue the physical labor of pastoral duties, Boyd began writing articles for a couple Christian publications, which led to him writing books, especially for children and new converts. Boyd found joy and hope in his writings, often receiving letters from people who had been changed by God after reading one of his books.

Robert Boyd's books were simple and plain and were used by God. D. L. Moody distributed thousands of copies of Boyd's *Glad Tidings* at his meetings in Great Britain, saying that he did not know of any better book for those seeking God. Charles Spurgeon recommended Boyd's book, *The World's Hope*. In addition to those two books, Boyd also authored *The Lives and Labors of Moody and Sankey, None but Christ Or the Sinner's Only Hope, Young Converts, Good News*, and others.

Despite Boyd's physical difficulties and his twelve years of being confined to bed and not being able to preach, he said, "God has given me such views of His character and gospel that I cannot be gloomy, much less despairing. Why should a living man complain, and especially a man in whom Christ lives by His Spirit, and to whom He says, *Because I live, ye shall live also*?"

Robert Boyd died at the end of August 1879, but his words live on.

Other Similar Titles

*The Pursuit of God,
by A. W. Tozer*

To have found God and still to pursue Him is a paradox of love, scorned indeed by the too-easily-satisfied religious person, but justified in happy experience by the children of the burning heart.

Come near to the holy men and women of the past and you will soon feel the heat of their desire after God. Let A. W. Tozer's pursuit of God spur you also into a genuine hunger and thirst to truly know God.

Available where books are sold.

*Jesus Came to Save Sinners,
by Charles H. Spurgeon*

This is a heart-level conversation with you, the reader. Every excuse, reason, and roadblock for not coming to Christ is examined and duly dealt with. If you think you may be too bad, or if perhaps you really are bad and you sin either openly or behind closed doors, you will discover that life in Christ is for you too. You can reject the message of salvation by faith, or you can choose to live a life of sin after professing faith in Christ, but you cannot change the truth as it is, either for yourself or for others. As such, it behooves you and your family to embrace truth, claim it for your own, and be genuinely set free for now and eternity. Come and embrace this free gift of God, and live a victorious life for Him.

Available where books are sold.

www.ingramcontent.com/pod-product-compliance
Lightning Source LLC
Chambersburg PA
CBHW070145080526
44586CB00015B/1849